The
BIBLE
Promise
Book®

*500 Scriptures for
Understanding
God's Grace*

The
BIBLE
Promise
Book®

500 Scriptures for Understanding God's Grace

Written and Compiled by
Jessie Fioritto

BARBOUR BOOKS
An Imprint of Barbour Publishing, Inc.

© 2019 by Barbour Publishing, Inc.

ISBN 978-1-68322-888-2

All scripture quotations are taken from the King James Version of the Bible.

Published by Barbour Books, an imprint of Barbour Publishing Inc., 1810 Barbour Drive, Uhrichsville, Ohio 44683, www.barbourbooks.com

Our mission is to inspire the world with the life-changing message of the Bible.

Member of the
Evangelical Christian
Publishers Association

Printed in the United States of America.

CONTENTS

ACCEPTED

Father in heaven, I don't have to hide my flaws and failures or clean myself up to come to You. I can come as I am with no fear that You will reject me. I've been cast aside by others, and it hurts. Their callous indifference threatened to strip me of my worth. But then I heard Your voice. You said, "Come." Anyone who asks will be forgiven. Your infinite grace covers all. You love me and welcome me because You created me. As a loving father You fold me in Your arms, and I am grateful. In Jesus' name I pray, amen.

1.

All that the Father giveth me shall come to me; and him that cometh to me I will in no wise cast out. For I came down from heaven, not to do mine own will, but the will of him that sent me.

JOHN 6:37–38

2.

Wherefore receive ye one another, as Christ also received us to the glory of God.

ROMANS 15:7

3.

But God commendeth his love toward us, in that, while we were yet sinners, Christ died for us. Much more then, being now justified by his blood, we shall be saved from wrath through him.

ROMANS 5:8–9

4.

But as many as received him, to them gave he power to become the sons of God, even to them that believe on his name: which were born, not of blood, nor of the will of the flesh, nor of the will of man, but of God.

JOHN 1:12–13

5.

Therefore being justified by faith, we have peace with God through our Lord Jesus Christ: by whom also we have access by faith into this grace wherein we stand, and rejoice in hope of the glory of God.

ROMANS 5:1–2

6.

And, having made peace through the blood of his cross, by him to reconcile all things unto himself; by him, I say, whether they be things in earth, or things in heaven. And you, that were sometime alienated and enemies in your mind by wicked works, yet now hath he reconciled in the body of his flesh through death, to present you holy and unblameable and unreproveable in his sight.

COLOSSIANS 1:20–22

7.

There is therefore now no condemnation to them which are in Christ Jesus, who walk not after the flesh, but after the Spirit.

ROMANS 8:1

8.

Sirs, what must I do to be saved? And they said, Believe on the Lord Jesus Christ, and thou shalt be saved, and thy house.

ACTS 16:30–31

9.

That if thou shalt confess with thy mouth
the Lord Jesus, and shalt believe in thine
heart that God hath raised him from the dead,
thou shalt be saved. For with the heart man
believeth unto righteousness; and with the
mouth confession is made unto salvation.

ROMANS 10:9–10

10.

Ye also, as lively stones, are built up a spiritual
house, an holy priesthood, to offer up spiritual
sacrifices, acceptable to God by Jesus Christ.

1 PETER 2:5

ADOPTED

Lord, You will adopt anyone who accepts the invitation to join Your family through faith in Jesus Christ. And this place in Your family is secure—forever! When I am overwhelmed by the cares of this world, remind me that I have a powerful Father who chose me to be His child. Show me that I am loved, protected, and provided with everything I need. Help me to respond in obedience, not trying to earn your blessing but simply because I am Your child. In the name of Jesus I pray, amen.

11.

Giving thanks unto the Father, which hath made us meet to be partakers of the inheritance of the saints in light: who hath delivered us from the power of darkness, and hath translated us into the kingdom of his dear Son.

Colossians 1:12–13

12.

But as many as received him, to them gave he power to become the sons of God, even to them that believe on his name: which were born, not of blood, nor of the will of the flesh, nor of the will of man, but of God.

John 1:12–13

13.

For as many as are led by the Spirit of God, they are
the sons of God. For ye have not received the spirit
of bondage again to fear; but ye have received the
Spirit of adoption, whereby we cry, Abba, Father.

Romans 8:14–15

14.

We are the children of God: and if children, then
heirs; heirs of God, and joint-heirs with Christ; if
so be that we suffer with him, that we may be also
glorified together. For I reckon that the sufferings
of this present time are not worthy to be compared
with the glory which shall be revealed in us.

Romans 8:16–18

15.

For we know that the whole creation groaneth
and travaileth in pain together until now. And
not only they, but ourselves also, which have the
firstfruits of the Spirit, even we ourselves groan
within ourselves, waiting for the adoption,
to wit, the redemption of our body.

Romans 8:22–23

16.

That ye may be blameless and harmless, the sons
of God, without rebuke, in the midst of a crooked
and perverse nation, among whom ye shine as
lights in the world; holding forth the word of life.

PHILIPPIANS 2:15–16

17.

Beloved, now are we the sons of God, and it
doth not yet appear what we shall be: but we
know that, when he shall appear, we shall be
like him; for we shall see him as he is.

1 JOHN 3:2

18.

For ye are all the children of God by faith in
Christ Jesus. For as many of you as have been
baptized into Christ have put on Christ.

GALATIANS 3:26–27

19.

But when the fulness of the time was come, God
sent forth his Son, made of a woman, made under
the law, to redeem them that were under the law,
that we might receive the adoption of sons.

GALATIANS 4:4–5

20.

He hath chosen us in him before the foundation
of the world, that we should be holy and without
blame before him in love: having predestinated
us unto the adoption of children by Jesus Christ
to himself, according to the good pleasure of his
will, to the praise of the glory of his grace, wherein
he hath made us accepted in the beloved.

EPHESIANS 1:4–6

ADORED

*Father, my human mind struggles to grasp the reality
that the almighty living God of the universe, Creator
of everything, delights in knowing me. And yet, it's so
easy for human parents to adore their own children.
Even through their flaws and bad days, parents can't get
enough of their kids. They want to know every facet of
their personalities, to share experiences with them, to
shower their parental affection on them. And You feel
that way for me! Your Word says that You sing over me
with joy. I want to know You better too, Lord. In Jesus'
name, amen.*

21.

The LORD thy God in the midst of thee is mighty; he
will save, he will rejoice over thee with joy; he will
rest in his love, he will joy over thee with singing.

ZEPHANIAH 3:17

22.

If ye then, being evil, know how to give
good gifts unto your children, how much
more shall your Father which is in heaven
give good things to them that ask him?

MATTHEW 7:11

23.

In my Father's house are many mansions: if it were
not so, I would have told you. I go to prepare a
place for you. And if I go and prepare a place
for you, I will come again, and receive you unto
myself; that where I am, there ye may be also.
And whither I go ye know, and the way ye know.

John 14:2–4

24.

They shall be abundantly satisfied with the fatness
of thy house; and thou shalt make them drink
of the river of thy pleasures. For with thee is the
fountain of life: in thy light shall we see light. O
continue thy lovingkindness unto them that know
thee; and thy righteousness to the upright in heart.

Psalm 36:8–10

25.

And God saw every thing that he had
made, and, behold, it was very good.

Genesis 1:31

26.

For God so loved the world, that he gave his
only begotten Son, that whosoever believeth
in him should not perish, but have everlasting
life. For God sent not his Son into the world
to condemn the world; but that the world
through him might be saved.

JOHN 3:16–17

27.

For I am persuaded, that neither death, nor
life, nor angels, nor principalities, nor powers,
nor things present, nor things to come, nor
height, nor depth, nor any other creature,
shall be able to separate us from the love of
God, which is in Christ Jesus our Lord.

ROMANS 8:38–39

28.

Are not two sparrows sold for a farthing?
and one of them shall not fall on the ground
without your Father. But the very hairs of your
head are all numbered. Fear ye not therefore,
ye are of more value than many sparrows.

MATTHEW 10:29–31

29.

But now in Christ Jesus ye who sometimes were far off are made nigh by the blood of Christ. For he is our peace, who hath made both one, and hath broken down the middle wall of partition between us.

EPHESIANS 2:13–14

30.

And I will walk among you, and will be your God, and ye shall be my people.

LEVITICUS 26:12

AMAZED

Lord God, I am in awe of You. Limitless is the word that describes every facet of You. Your power and knowledge, mercy and grace, goodness and justice know no borders. You are forever. Your Word says that You are the Alpha and Omega—who is and who was and who is to come— the Almighty, the beginning and the end. There is no God beside You! You hold eternity in the palm of Your hand, Father, and yet You still notice me. Although I am unworthy of Your regard, You freely offered me the water of life. Thank You, Lord, in Jesus' name. Amen.

31.

And he said unto me, It is done. I am Alpha and Omega, the beginning and the end. I will give unto him that is athirst of the fountain of the water of life freely. He that overcometh shall inherit all things; and I will be his God, and he shall be my son.

Revelation 21:6–7

32.

He hath made the earth by his power, he hath established the world by his wisdom, and hath stretched out the heavens by his discretion.

Jeremiah 10:12

33.

Thus saith the LORD the King of Israel, and his
redeemer the LORD of hosts; I am the first, and
I am the last; and beside me there is no God.
And who, as I, shall call, and shall declare it,
and set it in order for me, since I appointed the
ancient people? and the things that are coming,
and shall come, let them shew unto them.

ISAIAH 44:6–7

34.

Thine, O LORD is the greatness, and the power,
and the glory, and the victory, and the majesty:
for all that is in the heaven and in the earth
is thine; thine is the kingdom, O LORD,
and thou art exalted as head above all.

1 CHRONICLES 29:11

35.

And what is the exceeding greatness of his power
to us-ward who believe, according to the working
of his mighty power, which he wrought in Christ,
when he raised him from the dead, and set him at
his own right hand in the heavenly places.

EPHESIANS 1:19–20

36.

In whom we have redemption through his
blood, even the forgiveness of sins: who is the
image of the invisible God, the firstborn of every
creature: for by him were all things created, that
are in heaven, and that are in earth, visible and
invisible, whether they be thrones, or dominions,
or principalities, or powers: all things were
created by him, and for him: and he is before all
things, and by him all things consist.

COLOSSIANS 1:14–17

37.

But Jesus beheld them, and said unto
them, With men this is impossible;
but with God all things are possible.

MATTHEW 19:26

38.

Who being the brightness of his glory, and the
express image of his person, and upholding
all things by the word of his power, when he
had by himself purged our sins, sat down on
the right hand of the Majesty on high.

HEBREWS 1:3

39.

Lo, these are parts of his ways: but how little
a portion is heard of him? but the thunder
of his power who can understand?

JOB 26:14

40.

He telleth the number of the stars; he calleth
them all by their names. Great is our Lord, and
of great power: his understanding is infinite.

PSALM 147:4–5

AWAKENED

Father God, before I knew You I was dead. I walked aimlessly through my life, drifting with selfish ambition as my only guide. I was enslaved by my desires and blind to Your purpose for me. But You found me, Jesus. You showed me a better way, and now I am alive! I have awakened to Your good plans for me. It's as if a blindfold has fallen from my eyes and suddenly I see You everywhere. I see You in Your creation, hear You in a child's laugh, and even feel You in my pain. I have found new meaning in living for You. Amen.

41.

Wherefore he saith, Awake thou that sleepest, and arise from the dead, and Christ shall give thee light.

EPHESIANS 5:14

42.

And that, knowing the time, that now it is high time to awake out of sleep: for now is our salvation nearer than when we believed. The night is far spent, the day is at hand: let us therefore cast off the works of darkness, and let us put on the armour of light.

ROMANS 13:11–12

43.

He that loveth not knoweth not God; for God is love. In this was manifested the love of God toward us, because that God sent his only begotten Son into the world, that we might live through him. Herein is love, not that we loved God, but that he loved us, and sent his Son to be the propitiation for our sins. Beloved, if God so loved us, we ought also to love one another.

1 John 4:8–11

44.

Jesus answered and said unto him, Verily, verily, I say unto thee, Except a man be born again, he cannot see the kingdom of God.

John 3:3

45.

Hast thou not known? hast thou not heard, that the everlasting God, the Lord, the Creator of the ends of the earth, fainteth not, neither is weary? there is no searching of his understanding.

Isaiah 40:28

46.

Lay not up for yourselves treasures upon
earth, where moth and rust doth corrupt,
and where thieves break through and steal:
but lay up for yourselves treasures in heaven,
where neither moth nor rust doth corrupt, and
where thieves do not break through nor steal.

MATTHEW 6:19–20

47.

And we have seen and do testify that the Father
sent the Son to be the Saviour of the world.
Whosoever shall confess that Jesus is the Son
of God, God dwelleth in him, and he in God.

1 JOHN 4:14–15

48.

They should seek the Lord, if haply they
might feel after him, and find him, though
he be not far from every one of us: for in
him we live, and move, and have our being.

ACTS 17:27–28

49.

Wilt thou not revive us again:
that thy people may rejoice in thee?

PSALM 85:6

50.

Not by works of righteousness which we
have done, but according to his mercy he
saved us, by the washing of regeneration,
and renewing of the Holy Ghost.

TITUS 3:5

BLESSED

God, complaining comes so easily to me. My perspective desperately needs an overhaul. I too often focus on my problems and all the things that are less than what I desire. But I have realized that I need to adopt an attitude of thanksgiving. Because while I allow one small snag to steal my joy, I miss the blessings flooding into my life. Even if my health is less than perfect, if I am breathing, I am alive. And I have spiritual life in You. I have hope and peace and love through Christ. I am rich beyond measure in You! Thank You, Lord. In Jesus' name, amen.

51.

And of his fulness have all we
received, and grace for grace.

JOHN 1:16

52.

Give, and it shall be given unto you; good
measure, pressed down, and shaken together,
and running over, shall men give into your
bosom. For with the same measure that ye mete
withal it shall be measured to you again.

LUKE 6:38

53.

Blessed be the God and Father of our Lord Jesus Christ, who hath blessed us with all spiritual blessings in heavenly places in Christ: according as he hath chosen us in him before the foundation of the world, that we should be holy and without blame before him in love.

EPHESIANS 1:3–4

54.

In whom ye also trusted, after that ye heard the word of truth, the gospel of your salvation: in whom also after that ye believed, ye were sealed with that holy Spirit of promise, which is the earnest of our inheritance until the redemption of the purchased possession, unto the praise of his glory.

EPHESIANS 1:13–14

55.

And God is able to make all grace abound toward you; that ye, always having all sufficiency in all things, may abound to every good work.

2 CORINTHIANS 9:8

56.

Blessed is he whose transgression is forgiven,
whose sin is covered. Blessed is the man
unto whom the Lᴏʀᴅ imputeth not iniquity,
and in whose spirit there is no guile.

Psᴀʟᴍ 32:1–2

57.

Be careful for nothing; but in every thing
by prayer and supplication with thanksgiving
let your requests be made known unto God.
And the peace of God, which passeth all
understanding, shall keep your hearts and
minds through Christ Jesus.

Pʜɪʟɪᴘᴘɪᴀɴs 4:6–7

58.

But my God shall supply all your need
according to his riches in glory by Christ
Jesus. Now unto God and our Father be
glory for ever and ever. Amen.

Pʜɪʟɪᴘᴘɪᴀɴs 4:19–20

59.

Happy is he that hath the God of Jacob for his help, whose hope is in the LORD his God.

PSALM 146:5

60.

Trust in the LORD, and do good; so shalt thou dwell in the land, and verily thou shalt be fed. Delight thyself also in the LORD: and he shall give thee the desires of thine heart. Commit thy way unto the LORD; trust also in him; and he shall bring it to pass.

PSALM 37:3–5

CALLED

Father, You have a plan and a purpose for my life. And You promise to work everything for good for those who love You and are called according to Your purpose. I hold to the truth of this promise when I'm tempted to slip down the slope of questioning why hard things happen to me. Instead I focus on Your good character. You are a good Father who loves me and weaves the threads of my life into Your intricate plan. You called me into a relationship with You through Your Son. In Jesus' name, amen.

61.

And we know that all things work together
for good to them that love God, to them who
are the called according to his purpose.

ROMANS 8:28

62.

I therefore, the prisoner of the Lord, beseech
you that ye walk worthy of the vocation
wherewith ye are called, with all lowliness
and meekness, with longsuffering, forbearing
one another in love; endeavouring to keep
the unity of the Spirit in the bond of peace.

EPHESIANS 4:1–3

63.

But now thus saith the LORD that created thee,
O Jacob, and he that formed thee, O Israel,
Fear not: for I have redeemed thee, I have
called thee by thy name; thou art mine.

ISAIAH 43:1

64.

Who hath saved us, and called us with
an holy calling, not according to our
works, but according to his own purpose
and grace, which was given us in
Christ Jesus before the world began.

2 TIMOTHY 1:9

65.

Being confident of this very thing, that he
which hath begun a good work in you will
perform it until the day of Jesus Christ.

PHILIPPIANS 1:6

66.

But as God hath distributed to every man,
as the Lord hath called every one, so let him
walk. And so ordain I in all churches.

1 CORINTHIANS 7:17

67.

Go ye therefore, and teach all nations,
baptizing them in the name of the Father,
and of the Son, and of the Holy Ghost:
teaching them to observe all things whatsoever
I have commanded you: and, lo, I am with you
always, even unto the end of the world. Amen.

MATTHEW 28:19–20

68.

But we are bound to give thanks alway to
God for you, brethren beloved of the Lord,
because God hath from the beginning chosen
you to salvation through sanctification of the
Spirit and belief of the truth: whereunto he
called you by our gospel, to the obtaining
of the glory of our Lord Jesus Christ.

2 THESSALONIANS 2:13–14

69.

But ye are a chosen generation, a royal
priesthood, an holy nation, a peculiar people;
that ye should shew forth the praises of
him who hath called you out of darkness
into his marvellous light.

1 PETER 2:9

70.

For we are his workmanship, created in Christ
Jesus unto good works, which God hath before
ordained that we should walk in them.

EPHESIANS 2:10

CALMED

*God, this earth is a tumultuous place. It's a frenzy of
emotions and circumstances that threaten to sweep us
away into upheaval. But when I start feeling frantic
anxiety rise within me, I look to You. You are the good
Shepherd who leads me beside still waters and restores
my soul. You are the Master who looks at my storm and
orders, "Be still." I have found lasting peace in trusting
You. You comfort my fears and soothe my anxiety. No
matter what befalls me in this life I am calm in Your
care. In the name of Jesus I pray, amen.*

71.

Behold the fowls of the air: for they sow not,
neither do they reap, nor gather into barns; yet
your heavenly Father feedeth them. Are ye not
much better than they? Which of you by taking
thought can add one cubit unto his stature?

MATTHEW 6:26–27

72.

Yea, though I walk through the valley of the
shadow of death, I will fear no evil: for thou art
with me; thy rod and thy staff they comfort me.

PSALM 23:4

73.

In the multitude of my thoughts within
me thy comforts delight my soul.

PSALM 94:19

74.

Humble yourselves therefore under the
mighty hand of God, that he may exalt
you in due time: casting all your care
upon him; for he careth for you.

1 PETER 5:6–7

75.

For I the LORD thy God will hold thy right
hand, saying unto thee, Fear not; I will help
thee. Fear not, thou worm Jacob, and ye
men of Israel; I will help thee, saith the LORD,
and thy redeemer, the Holy One of Israel.

ISAIAH 41:13–14

76.

He that dwelleth in the secret place of the
most High shall abide under the shadow of the
Almighty. I will say of the LORD, He is my refuge
and my fortress: my God; in him will I trust.

PSALM 91:1–2

77.

Be careful for nothing; but in every thing
by prayer and supplication with thanksgiving
let your requests be made known unto God.
And the peace of God, which passeth all
understanding, shall keep your hearts
and minds through Christ Jesus.

PHILIPPIANS 4:6–7

78.

Peace I leave with you, my peace I give unto you:
not as the world giveth, give I unto you. Let not
your heart be troubled, neither let it be afraid.

JOHN 14:27

79.

What time I am afraid, I will trust in thee. In God
I will praise his word, in God I have put my trust;
I will not fear what flesh can do unto me.

PSALM 56:3–4

80.

Cast thy burden upon the LORD,
and he shall sustain thee: he shall
never suffer the righteous to be moved.

PSALM 55:22

CARED FOR

Father, why do I allow worries and fears to run me ragged when I am resting in the care of the good Shepherd—the One who loves me more than I could ever imagine or comprehend? You notice when a sparrow falls and have numbered the hairs on my head. You supply everything that I need, exactly when I need it. You tenderly carry the little lambs on Your shoulders. I want to trust You more. You're pleased to give good things to Your children, Father. And I am Your beloved child. Thank You for taking care of every aspect of my life. In Jesus' name, amen.

81.

But my God shall supply all your need
according to his riches in glory by Christ
Jesus. Now unto God and our Father
be glory for ever and ever. Amen.

<small>Philippians 4:19–20</small>

82.

Cast thy burden upon the Lord,
and he shall sustain thee: he shall
never suffer the righteous to be moved.

<small>Psalm 55:22</small>

83.

And this is the confidence that we have in him,
that, if we ask any thing according to his will,
he heareth us: and if we know that he hear us,
whatsoever we ask, we know that we have
the petitions that we desired of him.

1 John 5:14–15

84.

Wherefore, if God so clothe the grass of the
field, which to day is, and to morrow is cast into
the oven, shall he not much more clothe you,
O ye of little faith? Therefore take no thought,
saying, What shall we eat? or, What shall we
drink? or, Wherewithal shall we be clothed?
(For after all these things do the Gentiles seek:)
for your heavenly Father knoweth that
ye have need of all these things.

Matthew 6:30–32

85.

The Lord is my shepherd; I shall not want.
He maketh me to lie down in green pastures:
he leadeth me beside the still waters.

Psalm 23:1–2

86.

I am poor and needy; yet the Lord thinketh
upon me: thou art my help and my deliverer;
make no tarrying, O my God.

PSALM 40:17

⸺⸻⸺

87.

Are not five sparrows sold for two farthings,
and not one of them is forgotten before God?
But even the very hairs of your head are all
numbered. Fear not therefore: ye are of
more value than many sparrows.

LUKE 12:6–7

⸺⸻⸺

88.

Behold, the Lord GOD will come with
strong hand, and his arm shall rule for him:
behold, his reward is with him, and his
work before him. He shall feed his flock like a
shepherd: he shall gather the lambs with his
arm, and carry them in his bosom, and shall
gently lead those that are with young.

ISAIAH 40:10–11

89.

Trust in the LORD, and do good; so shalt thou dwell in the land, and verily thou shalt be fed. Delight thyself also in the LORD: and he shall give thee the desires of thine heart.

PSALM 37:3–4

90.

The thief cometh not, but for to steal, and to kill, and to destroy: I am come that they might have life, and that they might have it more abundantly. I am the good shepherd: the good shepherd giveth his life for the sheep.

JOHN 10:10–11

CELEBRATED

*Lord, people are thrilled to celebrate their children's
accomplishments, even if it is only the feat of growing a
year older. We throw parties and give gifts and eat cake
and laugh. We are so overjoyed at our children's success.
How could we think that You would not celebrate us,
Your children? Your Word says that there's more joy
in heaven over one repentant sinner than over all the
righteous—and that You rejoice over us with singing.
You love us and experience indescribable joy when we
are born into Your kingdom. Thank You, Father. In the
name of Jesus, amen.*

91.

Thou wilt shew me the path of life: in thy
presence is fulness of joy; at thy right
hand there are pleasures for evermore.

PSALM 16:11

92.

Let them praise his name in the dance: let them
sing praises unto him with the timbrel and harp.
For the LORD taketh pleasure in his people:
he will beautify the meek with salvation.

PSALM 149:3–4

93.

When he cometh home, he calleth together
his friends and neighbours, saying unto them,
Rejoice with me; for I have found my sheep
which was lost. I say unto you, that likewise joy
shall be in heaven over one sinner that repenteth,
more than over ninety and nine just persons,
which need no repentance.

Luke 15:6–7

94.

And God saw every thing that he had made,
and, behold, it was very good. And the
evening and the morning were the sixth day.

Genesis 1:31

95.

The Lord thy God in the midst of thee is
mighty; he will save, he will rejoice over
thee with joy; he will rest in his love,
he will joy over thee with singing.

Zephaniah 3:17

96.

These things have I spoken unto you,
that my joy might remain in you,
and that your joy might be full.

JOHN 15:11

97.

Bring forth the best robe, and put it on him;
and put a ring on his hand, and shoes on his
feet: and bring hither the fatted calf, and kill
it; and let us eat, and be merry: for this my
son was dead, and is alive again; he was lost,
and is found. And they began to be merry.

LUKE 15:22–24

98.

For as a young man marrieth a virgin,
so shall thy sons marry thee: and as the
bridegroom rejoiceth over the bride,
so shall thy God rejoice over thee.

ISAIAH 62:5

99.

In my Father's house are many mansions: if it
were not so, I would have told you. I go to prepare
a place for you. And if I go and prepare a place
for you, I will come again, and receive you unto
myself; that where I am, there ye may be also.

JOHN 14:2–3

100.

Let us be glad and rejoice, and give honour
to him: for the marriage of the Lamb is come,
and his wife hath made herself ready. And to
her was granted that she should be arrayed
in fine linen, clean and white: for the fine
linen is the righteousness of saints.

REVELATION 19:7–8

CHALLENGED

*Lord, You challenge those who would be Your disciples
to take up their crosses and follow You daily. You've
told me that if I want to save my life I must lose it. So
I have enslaved myself to righteousness. I choose You,
Jesus. The world doesn't understand why I would give
up myself to serve You. Surrender can be excruciating,
just as Calvary was for You. Dying to my own pride
and selfishness is hard. But You promise me something
so much greater. I have given my life to You, and You
have given me back eternity and abundant life today. In
Jesus' name, amen.*

101.
Present your bodies a living sacrifice,
holy, acceptable unto God, which is your
reasonable service. And be not conformed
to this world: but be ye transformed by the
renewing of your mind, that ye may prove
what is that good, and acceptable,
and perfect, will of God.
ROMANS 12:1–2

102.

And he said to them all, If any man will come after me, let him deny himself, and take up his cross daily, and follow me. For whosoever will save his life shall lose it: but whosoever will lose his life for my sake, the same shall save it.

Luke 9:23–24

103.

And he went a little farther, and fell on his face, and prayed, saying, O my Father, if it be possible, let this cup pass from me: nevertheless not as I will, but as thou wilt.

Matthew 26:39

104.

Know ye not that your body is the temple of the Holy Ghost which is in you, which ye have of God, and ye are not your own? For ye are bought with a price: therefore glorify God in your body, and in your spirit, which are God's.

1 Corinthians 6:19–20

105.

Thou shalt love the Lord thy God with all
thy heart, and with all thy soul, and with
all thy strength, and with all thy mind;
and thy neighbour as thyself.

LUKE 10:27

106.

Submit yourselves therefore to God. Resist
the devil, and he will flee from you. Draw
nigh to God, and he will draw nigh to you.
Cleanse your hands, ye sinners; and purify
your hearts, ye double minded.

JAMES 4:7–8

107.

Abide in me, and I in you. As the branch cannot
bear fruit of itself, except it abide in the vine;
no more can ye, except ye abide in me. I am the
vine, ye are the branches: He that abideth in me,
and I in him, the same bringeth forth much fruit:
for without me ye can do nothing.

JOHN 15:4–5

108.

Let this mind be in you, which was also in
Christ Jesus: who, being in the form of God,
thought it not robbery to be equal with God:
but made himself of no reputation, and took
upon him the form of a servant.

PHILIPPIANS 2:5–7

109.

I am crucified with Christ: nevertheless I live; yet
not I, but Christ liveth in me: and the life which I
now live in the flesh I live by the faith of the Son
of God, who loved me, and gave himself for me.

GALATIANS 2:20

110.

Go ye therefore, and teach all nations,
baptizing them in the name of the Father,
and of the Son, and of the Holy Ghost:
teaching them to observe all things whatsoever
I have commanded you: and, lo, I am with
you always, even unto the end of the world.

MATTHEW 28:19–20

CHERISHED

Lord, I am in awe that the spectacular God of all would notice me. You see the past, present, and future, and yet You still see me in the midst of this vast universe. And not only do You notice me, but You place great value on me. So much so that You would die for me. I am held dear by You and showered with Your affection. No matter what happens to me here, whether I am mistreated or hurt, I rest in the knowledge that I am cherished by You, my loving Father in heaven. In Jesus' name I pray, amen.

111.

For no man ever yet hated his own flesh;
but nourisheth and cherisheth it, even as
the Lord the church: for we are members
of his body, of his flesh, and of his bones.

EPHESIANS 5:29–30

112.

Thou art all fair, my love;
there is no spot in thee.

SONG OF SOLOMON 4:7

113.

The LORD hath appeared of old unto me, saying,
Yea, I have loved thee with an everlasting love:
therefore with lovingkindness have I drawn thee.
Again I will build thee, and thou shalt be built,
O virgin of Israel: thou shalt again be adorned
with thy tabrets, and shalt go forth in the
dances of them that make merry.

JEREMIAH 31:3–4

114.

But God, who is rich in mercy, for his great
love wherewith he loved us, even when we
were dead in sins, hath quickened us together
with Christ, (by grace ye are saved).

EPHESIANS 2:4–5

115.

For the mountains shall depart, and the hills be
removed; but my kindness shall not depart from
thee, neither shall the covenant of my peace be
removed, saith the LORD that hath mercy on thee.

ISAIAH 54:10

116.

In this was manifested the love of God
toward us, because that God sent his only
begotten Son into the world, that we might
live through him. Herein is love, not that
we loved God, but that he loved us, and sent
his Son to be the propitiation for our sins.

1 John 4:9–10

117.

Can a woman forget her sucking child, that she
should not have compassion on the son of her
womb? yea, they may forget, yet will I not forget
thee. Behold, I have graven thee upon the palms
of my hands; thy walls are continually before me.

Isaiah 49:15–16

118.

But as many as received him, to them gave
he power to become the sons of God,
even to them that believe on his name.

John 1:12

119.

For I am the LORD thy God, the Holy One of
Israel, thy Saviour: I gave Egypt for thy ransom,
Ethiopia and Seba for thee. Since thou wast
precious in my sight, thou hast been honourable,
and I have loved thee: therefore will I give
men for thee, and people for thy life.

ISAIAH 43:3–4

120.

Are not five sparrows sold for two farthings,
and not one of them is forgotten before God?
But even the very hairs of your head are all
numbered. Fear not therefore: ye are of
more value than many sparrows.

LUKE 12:6–7

CHOSEN

Lord, for some strange reason You've chosen us—all of us measly and ungrateful sinners—to be part of Your family. You called us out of our darkness and into the marvelous light of Your grace. You are the spectacular God who is capable of making things that are not come into being. We were scattered and You gathered us into a holy family; we were condemned and You pardoned us with mercy. You picked me, and all I have to do is choose You back. I choose You! In the name of Jesus, amen.

121.

But ye are a chosen generation, a royal priest-hood, an holy nation, a peculiar people; that ye should shew forth the praises of him who hath called you out of darkness into his marvellous light; which in time past were not a people, but are now the people of God: which had not obtained mercy, but now have obtained mercy.

1 PETER 2:9–10

122.

Ye are all one in Christ Jesus. And if ye be Christ's, then are ye Abraham's seed, and heirs according to the promise.

GALATIANS 3:28–29

123.

Ye have not chosen me, but I have chosen you, and ordained you, that ye should go and bring forth fruit, and that your fruit should remain: that whatsoever ye shall ask of the Father in my name, he may give it you.

JOHN 15:16

124.

Because the foolishness of God is wiser than men; and the weakness of God is stronger than men. For ye see your calling, brethren, how that not many wise men after the flesh, not many mighty, not many noble, are called.

1 CORINTHIANS 1:25–26

125.

Blessed be the God and Father of our Lord Jesus Christ, who hath blessed us with all spiritual blessings in heavenly places in Christ: according as he hath chosen us in him before the foundation of the world, that we should be holy and without blame before him in love.

EPHESIANS 1:3–4

126.

But we are bound to give thanks alway to
God for you, brethren beloved of the Lord,
because God hath from the beginning chosen
you to salvation through sanctification of
the Spirit and belief of the truth.

2 THESSALONIANS 2:13

127.

Thou therefore endure hardness, as a good soldier
of Jesus Christ. No man that warreth entangleth
himself with the affairs of this life; that he may
please him who hath chosen him to be a soldier.

2 TIMOTHY 2:3–4

128.

Hearken, my beloved brethren, Hath not
God chosen the poor of this world rich in
faith, and heirs of the kingdom which he
hath promised to them that love him?

JAMES 2:5

129.

These shall make war with the Lamb, and the
Lamb shall overcome them: for he is Lord of
lords, and King of kings: and they that are with
him are called, and chosen, and faithful.

REVELATION 17:14

130.

Having predestinated us unto the adoption of
children by Jesus Christ to himself, according
to the good pleasure of his will, to the praise
of the glory of his grace, wherein he hath
made us accepted in the beloved.

EPHESIANS 1:5–6

CLEANSED

Father in heaven, I feel the filth of my sin. I know the shame that comes with being considered dirty and unworthy. I've knowingly done things that are wrong. But You have plunged me into a clear spring of water. Your Son's blood has scoured away all of my sin. I no longer hide my ratty rags in the darkness. Instead I step into the light and come closer to You, assured by my faith in You that I have been washed and purified. My conscience is clean! In Jesus' name, amen.

131.
Let us draw near with a true heart in
full assurance of faith, having our hearts
sprinkled from an evil conscience,
and our bodies washed with pure water.

HEBREWS 10:22

132.
But if we walk in the light, as he is in
the light, we have fellowship one with
another, and the blood of Jesus Christ
his Son cleanseth us from all sin.

1 JOHN 1:7

133.

Now ye are clean through the word which I have
spoken unto you. Abide in me, and I in you.

JOHN 15:3–4

134.

And such were some of you: but ye are
washed, but ye are sanctified, but ye are
justified in the name of the Lord Jesus,
and by the Spirit of our God.

1 CORINTHIANS 6:11

135.

Have mercy upon me, O God, according to thy
lovingkindness: according unto the multitude of
thy tender mercies blot out my transgressions.
Wash me throughly from mine iniquity, and
cleanse me from my sin.

PSALM 51:1–2

136.

If we confess our sins, he is faithful and just to forgive us our sins, and to cleanse us from all unrighteousness.

1 JOHN 1:9

137.

For on that day shall the priest make an atonement for you, to cleanse you, that ye may be clean from all your sins before the LORD.

LEVITICUS 16:30

138.

And I will cleanse them from all their iniquity, whereby they have sinned against me; and I will pardon all their iniquities, whereby they have sinned, and whereby they have transgressed against me.

JEREMIAH 33:8

139.

Hide thy face from my sins, and blot out all mine iniquities. Create in me a clean heart, O God; and renew a right spirit within me.

PSALM 51:9–10

140.

Who gave himself for us, that he might redeem us from all iniquity, and purify unto himself a peculiar people, zealous of good works.

TITUS 2:14

COMFORTED

Father, a child cries out in the night. A parent's instinct is to shush and cuddle, to sing, to assure—to comfort. We want to ease their angst or pain and calm their fears, to restore rightness to their world and bring peace to their little minds. And at times I need all of these assurances too. I know that when I walk through the dark valleys, Your presence will comfort me. I am sheltered under the shadow of Your mighty wings, held close to Your side. Your peace that passes all understanding soothes my mind and heart. In Jesus' name, amen.

141.

As one whom his mother comforteth, so will
I comfort you; and ye shall be comforted in
Jerusalem. And when ye see this, your heart shall
rejoice, and your bones shall flourish like an herb.

ISAIAH 66:13–14

142.

Yea, though I walk through the valley of the shadow
of death, I will fear no evil: for thou art with me;
thy rod and thy staff they comfort me.

PSALM 23:4

143.

Blessed be God, even the Father of our Lord
Jesus Christ, the Father of mercies, and the
God of all comfort; who comforteth us in all
our tribulation, that we may be able to comfort
them which are in any trouble, by the comfort
wherewith we ourselves are comforted of God.

2 Corinthians 1:3–4

144.

Then had the churches rest throughout all
Judaea and Galilee and Samaria, and were edified;
and walking in the fear of the Lord, and in the
comfort of the Holy Ghost, were multiplied.

Acts 9:31

145.

Blessed are they that mourn:
for they shall be comforted.

Matthew 5:4

146.

Thou shalt increase my greatness,
and comfort me on every side.

PSALM 71:21

147.

And in that day thou shalt say, O LORD,
I will praise thee: though thou wast angry
with me, thine anger is turned away, and thou
comfortedst me. Behold, God is my salvation.

ISAIAH 12:1–2

148.

Sing, O heavens; and be joyful, O earth;
and break forth into singing, O mountains:
for the LORD hath comforted his people,
and will have mercy upon his afflicted.

ISAIAH 49:13

149.

He healeth the broken in heart,
and bindeth up their wounds.

PSALM 147:3

150.

Now our Lord Jesus Christ himself, and God,
even our Father, which hath loved us, and hath
given us everlasting consolation and good hope
through grace, comfort your hearts, and stablish
you in every good word and work.

2 THESSALONIANS 2:16–17

COMMISSIONED

God, my life has been infused with new purpose. I no longer wander this world wondering what it's all about and searching for the point of living. You've commissioned me into Your army and given me an assignment to fulfill with the days that I walk this earth. My mission is to make disciples for You—to live in such a way before all who see my life that Your kingdom is glorified. I pray that You would keep me from distraction and shield me from the enemy's attacks so I can work in Your harvest. In the name of Jesus, amen.

151.

Go ye therefore, and teach all nations, baptizing them in the name of the Father, and of the Son, and of the Holy Ghost: teaching them to observe all things whatsoever I have commanded you: and, lo, I am with you always, even unto the end of the world. Amen.

MATTHEW 28:19–20

152.

And he said unto them, Go ye into all the world, and preach the gospel to every creature.

MARK 16:15

153.

And the things that thou hast heard of me among many witnesses, the same commit thou to faithful men, who shall be able to teach others also. Thou therefore endure hardness, as a good soldier of Jesus Christ.

2 TIMOTHY 2:2–3

154.

Brethren, if any of you do err from the truth, and one convert him; let him know, that he which converteth the sinner from the error of his way shall save a soul from death, and shall hide a multitude of sins.

JAMES 5:19–20

155.

If ye walk in my statutes, and keep my commandments, and do them; then I will give you rain in due season, and the land shall yield her increase, and the trees of the field shall yield their fruit.

LEVITICUS 26:3–4

156.

Let the word of Christ dwell in you richly in all
wisdom; teaching and admonishing one another
in psalms and hymns and spiritual songs, singing
with grace in your hearts to the Lord.

COLOSSIANS 3:16

157.

Then said Jesus to them again, Peace be unto you:
as my Father hath sent me, even so send I you.
And when he had said this, he breathed on them,
and saith unto them, Receive ye the Holy Ghost.

JOHN 20:21–22

158.

But ye shall receive power, after that the
Holy Ghost is come upon you: and ye shall
be witnesses unto me both in Jerusalem,
and in all Judaea, and in Samaria, and unto
the uttermost part of the earth.

ACTS 1:8

159.

And how shall they preach, except they be sent? as it is written, How beautiful are the feet of them that preach the gospel of peace, and bring glad tidings of good things!

ROMANS 10:15

160.

Then saith he unto his disciples, The harvest truly is plenteous, but the labourers are few; pray ye therefore the Lord of the harvest, that he will send forth labourers into his harvest.

MATTHEW 9:37–38

DELIVERED

God, I stand before You a guilty person, convicted by Your law of innumerable transgressions. There is no doubt that I committed them all—I'm guilty on all counts. No jury would ever let me go free. An eternal prison of separation from You gapes hungrily in my future. But then Jesus steps in front of me, saying that I belong to Him and that He has already paid my penalty. He takes my hand and delivers me from a death sentence into life. From the pit into paradise eternal. Thank You, Jesus! Amen.

161.

Giving thanks unto the Father, which hath made us meet to be partakers of the inheritance of the saints in light: who hath delivered us from the power of darkness, and hath translated us into the kingdom of his dear Son.

Colossians 1:12–13

162.

But God commendeth his love toward us, in that, while we were yet sinners, Christ died for us.

Romans 5:8

163.
Be ye reconciled to God. For he hath made him
to be sin for us, who knew no sin; that we might
be made the righteousness of God in him.

2 Corinthians 5:20–21

164.
Blessed are the poor in spirit: for theirs is
the kingdom of heaven. Blessed are they that
mourn: for they shall be comforted. Blessed are
the meek: for they shall inherit the earth.

Matthew 5:3–5

165.
And be found in him, not having mine own
righteousness, which is of the law, but that
which is through the faith of Christ, the
righteousness which is of God by faith.

Philippians 3:9

166.

For the wages of sin is death; but the gift of God
is eternal life through Jesus Christ our Lord.

Romans 6:23

167.

For if by one man's offence death reigned by
one; much more they which receive abundance
of grace and of the gift of righteousness shall
reign in life by one, Jesus Christ.

Romans 5:17

168.

Our old man is crucified with him,
that the body of sin might be destroyed,
that henceforth we should not serve sin.
For he that is dead is freed from sin.

Romans 6:6–7

169.

Stand fast therefore in the liberty wherewith
Christ hath made us free, and be not entangled
again with the yoke of bondage.

GALATIANS 5:1

170.

He that hath the Son hath life; and he that
hath not the Son of God hath not life. These
things have I written unto you that believe
on the name of the Son of God; that ye may
know that ye have eternal life, and that ye may
believe on the name of the Son of God.

1 JOHN 5:12–13

EMPOWERED

Father, I know that I can't do this Christian life on my own. I've tried and I've failed miserably to do the right thing. My spirit is willing but my flesh is oh so weak. But I have a supernatural power source: Your Holy Spirit dwelling in me. The same power that created the universe. The same magnificent power that both drives hurricanes and stills storms with a word—the fullness of God's mighty power—lives within me. All I have to do is ask for Your help. You give me the strength to be an overcomer. In the name of Jesus, amen.

171.

But ye shall receive power, after that
the Holy Ghost is come upon you.

ACTS 1:8

172.

Whereby are given unto us exceeding great and
precious promises: that by these ye might be
partakers of the divine nature, having escaped the
corruption that is in the world through lust.

2 PETER 1:4

173.
I can do all things through Christ
which strengtheneth me.
PHILIPPIANS 4:13

174.
That I may know him, and the power of his
resurrection, and the fellowship of his sufferings,
being made conformable unto his death.
PHILIPPIANS 3:10

175.
Grace and peace be multiplied unto you
through the knowledge of God, and of Jesus
our Lord, according as his divine power hath
given unto us all things that pertain unto life
and godliness, through the knowledge of him
that hath called us to glory and virtue.
2 PETER 1:2–3

176.

For whatsoever is born of God overcometh
the world: and this is the victory that
overcometh the world, even our faith.

1 John 5:4

177.

For we have not followed cunningly devised
fables, when we made known unto you the
power and coming of our Lord Jesus Christ,
but were eyewitnesses of his majesty.

2 Peter 1:16

178.

There hath no temptation taken you but such as
is common to man: but God is faithful, who will
not suffer you to be tempted above that ye are
able; but will with the temptation also make a
way to escape, that ye may be able to bear it.

1 Corinthians 10:13

179.

Confess your faults one to another, and pray one
for another, that ye may be healed. The effectual
fervent prayer of a righteous man availeth much.

JAMES 5:16

180.

For God hath not given us the spirit of fear;
but of power, and of love, and of a sound mind.

2 TIMOTHY 1:7

ENCOURAGED

*God, just when it looks like the good guys are positioned
for ultimate failure, my favorite superhero charges
onto the screen. Who doesn't love a good fantasy? They
encourage us to strive for more in our own lives—more
courage, more honor, more strength. It's fun to imagine
new worlds, but in the end they're not real. The Bible,
though, is not just another collection of fairy tales. You
use every word to lift my spirits and spur me toward
hope and endurance. I am encouraged by Your daring
story of love and sacrifice, and by my hero, Jesus. Amen.*

181.
For whatsoever things were written aforetime
were written for our learning, that we
through patience and comfort of the
scriptures might have hope.
ROMANS 15:4

182.
These things I have spoken unto you, that
in me ye might have peace. In the world
ye shall have tribulation: but be of good
cheer; I have overcome the world.
JOHN 16:33

183.

For God hath not appointed us to wrath,
but to obtain salvation by our Lord Jesus
Christ, who died for us, that, whether we wake
or sleep, we should live together with him.
Wherefore comfort yourselves together, and
edify one another, even as also ye do.

1 THESSALONIANS 5:9–11

184.

Every word of God is pure: he is a shield
unto them that put their trust in him.

PROVERBS 30:5

185.

For I know the thoughts that I think toward
you, saith the LORD, thoughts of peace,
and not of evil, to give you an expected end.

JEREMIAH 29:11

186.

I will lift up mine eyes unto the hills, from
whence cometh my help. My help cometh
from the LORD, which made heaven and earth.

PSALM 121:1–2

187.

The LORD is my strength and my shield;
my heart trusted in him, and I am helped:
therefore my heart greatly rejoiceth;
and with my song will I praise him.

PSALM 28:7

188.

And let us consider one another to provoke
unto love and to good works: not forsaking the
assembling of ourselves together, as the manner
of some is; but exhorting one another: and so
much the more, as ye see the day approaching.

HEBREWS 10:24–25

189.

And ye shall seek me, and find me, when ye
shall search for me with all your heart.

JEREMIAH 29:13

190.

For our light affliction, which is but for a
moment, worketh for us a far more exceeding and
eternal weight of glory; while we look not at the
things which are seen, but at the things which are
not seen: for the things which are seen are tempo-
ral; but the things which are not seen are eternal.

2 CORINTHIANS 4:17–18

FILLED

Lord, we're always searching for beauty. We're attracted to things that are pleasing and soothing to our battered senses. We fill our gardens with exotic blooms and trickling water features to create an atmosphere of serenity. And the sensory pleasure of a waterfall is experienced only when the pool overflows. As the psalmist wrote, "my cup runneth over." You have filled me with Your love, Your grace, Your joy, Your unsurpassed peace until it flows over my brim, delighting all those around me. My spirit is no longer empty, instead I am filled with Your fullness. In Jesus' name, amen.

191.

My cup runneth over.

PSALM 23:5

192.

And Ananias went his way, and entered into
the house; and putting his hands on him said,
Brother Saul, the Lord, even Jesus, that appeared
unto thee in the way as thou camest, hath
sent me, that thou mightest receive thy sight,
and be filled with the Holy Ghost.

ACTS 9:17

193.

Now the God of hope fill you with all joy and
peace in believing, that ye may abound in hope,
through the power of the Holy Ghost.

ROMANS 15:13

194.

Blessed are they which do hunger and thirst
after righteousness: for they shall be filled.

MATTHEW 5:6

195.

And they were all filled with the Holy Ghost,
and began to speak with other tongues,
as the Spirit gave them utterance.

ACTS 2:4

196.

For by one Spirit are we all baptized into
one body, whether we be Jews or Gentiles,
whether we be bond or free; and have been
all made to drink into one Spirit.

1 CORINTHIANS 12:13

197.

But ye are not in the flesh, but in the Spirit,
if so be that the Spirit of God dwell in you.

ROMANS 8:9

198.

And hope maketh not ashamed; because the
love of God is shed abroad in our hearts by
the Holy Ghost which is given unto us.

ROMANS 5:5

199.

My soul shall be satisfied as with marrow
and fatness; and my mouth shall
praise thee with joyful lips.

PSALM 63:5

200.

And the LORD shall guide thee continually, and
satisfy thy soul in drought, and make fat thy
bones: and thou shalt be like a watered garden,
and like a spring of water, whose waters fail not.

ISAIAH 58:11

FORGIVEN

Lord, I had this unbearable load of guilt and shame pressing down on me. There was no relief or escape from its condemning weight. I tried to ignore it and rationalize it away—after all, I'm no worse than anyone else, right? I did a lot of good things too. But always the burden returned, because I was guilty. No number of good deeds could ease the screaming of my conscience. But then You took the guilt from me. I asked and You lifted away the load as if it had never been. You told me to go in peace, for my sins were forgiven. Wiped away clean! Thank You, Lord. Amen.

201.
If we confess our sins, he is faithful
and just to forgive us our sins, and to
cleanse us from all unrighteousness.

1 John 1:9

202.
Forbearing one another, and forgiving one
another, if any man have a quarrel against any:
even as Christ forgave you, so also do ye.

Colossians 3:13

203.

He hath not dealt with us after our sins;
nor rewarded us according to our iniquities.
For as the heaven is high above the earth,
so great is his mercy toward them that fear him.
As far as the east is from the west, so far hath
he removed our transgressions from us.

PSALM 103:10–12

204.

Then Peter said unto them, Repent, and be
baptized every one of you in the name of
Jesus Christ for the remission of sins, and ye
shall receive the gift of the Holy Ghost.

ACTS 2:38

205.

For if ye forgive men their trespasses,
your heavenly Father will also forgive you.

MATTHEW 6:14

206.

I acknowledge my sin unto thee, and
mine iniquity have I not hid. I said, I will
confess my transgressions unto the LORD;
and thou forgavest the iniquity of my sin.

PSALM 32:5

207.

For this is my blood of the new testament,
which is shed for many for the remission of sins.

MATTHEW 26:28

208.

Wherefore I say unto thee, Her sins, which are
many, are forgiven; for she loved much: but to
whom little is forgiven, the same loveth little.
And he said unto her, Thy sins are forgiven.

LUKE 7:47–48

209.

In whom we have redemption through
his blood, the forgiveness of sins,
according to the riches of his grace.

EPHESIANS 1:7

210.

Repent ye therefore, and be converted,
that your sins may be blotted out,
when the times of refreshing shall come
from the presence of the Lord.

ACTS 3:19

FREED

Father, I think of a puppy confined to a cage while its family is away—she's lonely and sad and longing for the opportunity to run freely like she was made to do. When her owners return and open the cage, she bolts through the door with wild abandon, totally exhilarated to be released from her confinement. That's kind of a picture of me, Lord. Before I met You I was chained to my sin and guilt. But You freed me from the shackles of my old life. You released me from my death sentence and threw open the prison gates. And I too sprinted into the glorious freedom of a new life with You. Thank You, in the name of Jesus. Amen.

211.

Stand fast therefore in the liberty wherewith
Christ hath made us free, and be not
entangled again with the yoke of bondage.

GALATIANS 5:1

212.

And ye shall know the truth,
and the truth shall make you free.

JOHN 8:32

213.

Being then made free from sin,
ye became the servants of righteousness.

ROMANS 6:18

214.

For, brethren, ye have been called unto
liberty; only use not liberty for an occasion
to the flesh, but by love serve one another.

GALATIANS 5:13

215.

There is therefore now no condemnation to
them which are in Christ Jesus, who walk not
after the flesh, but after the Spirit. For the law
of the Spirit of life in Christ Jesus hath made
me free from the law of sin and death.

ROMANS 8:1–2

216.

The Spirit of the Lord GOD is upon me;
because the LORD hath anointed me to
preach good tidings unto the meek; he hath
sent me to bind up the brokenhearted, to
proclaim liberty to the captives, and the
opening of the prison to them that are bound.

ISAIAH 61:1

217.

Because the creature itself also shall be
delivered from the bondage of corruption into
the glorious liberty of the children of God.

ROMANS 8:21

218.

Is not this the fast that I have chosen? to loose
the bands of wickedness, to undo the heavy
burdens, and to let the oppressed go free,
and that ye break every yoke?

ISAIAH 58:6

219.

For though I be free from all men,
yet have I made myself servant unto
all, that I might gain the more.

1 CORINTHIANS 9:19

220.

Who is he that overcometh the world, but he
that believeth that Jesus is the Son of God?

1 JOHN 5:5

GUIDED

*Lord, early American settlers heading west hired trail
guides to lead them safely across the vast wilderness.
These guides knew where to find water and how to
avoid dangers—and most importantly they knew
how to get where they were going. Father, there's great
comfort in following someone who knows the way
through treacherous territory. You lead me to living
water and teach me to avoid the enemy's traps.
When I follow You, You keep my feet from stumbling.
Show me the way You want me to go and keep me from
being distracted by false trails. In Jesus' name, amen.*

221.

Jesus saith unto him, I am the way,
the truth, and the life: no man cometh
unto the Father, but by me.

JOHN 14:6

222.

Beloved, believe not every spirit, but try the
spirits whether they are of God: because many
false prophets are gone out into the world.

1 JOHN 4:1

223.

Thy word is a lamp unto my feet,
and a light unto my path.

Psalm 119:105

224.

All scripture is given by inspiration of God,
and is profitable for doctrine, for reproof,
for correction, for instruction in righteousness.

2 Timothy 3:16

225.

But whoso keepeth his word, in him verily is the
love of God perfected: hereby know we that we
are in him. He that saith he abideth in him ought
himself also so to walk, even as he walked.

1 John 2:5–6

226.

The angel of the Lord encampeth round about
them that fear him, and delivereth them.

Psalm 34:7

227.

Fear thou not; for I am with thee: be not
dismayed; for I am thy God: I will strengthen
thee; yea, I will help thee; yea, I will uphold
thee with the right hand of my righteousness.

Isaiah 41:10

228.

Though I walk in the midst of trouble,
thou wilt revive me: thou shalt stretch
forth thine hand against the wrath of mine
enemies, and thy right hand shall save me.

Psalm 138:7

229.

The LORD is my shepherd; I shall not want.
He maketh me to lie down in green pastures:
he leadeth me beside the still waters.

PSALM 23:1–2

230.

The LORD shall preserve thee from all evil:
he shall preserve thy soul. The LORD shall
preserve thy going out and thy coming in
from this time forth, and even for evermore.

PSALM 121:7–8

HEALED

*Lord, You didn't have to heal diseases and mend bodies
when You walked here on earth. It would have been
enough for You to come and grant us grace through Your
blood. You didn't have to raise the dead and remove
discomfort. But You did. Because You love us. You are
the Great Physician, the Ultimate Healer. And not
only can You heal broken bodies, You can mend broken
hearts. You have wrapped my battered soul in the
tender bindings of Your love and mercy. You've healed
me of my guilt and shame. In the name of Jesus, amen.*

231.
Who his own self bare our sins in his
own body on the tree, that we, being dead
to sins, should live unto righteousness:
by whose stripes ye were healed.
1 Peter 2:24

232.
Then shall thy light break forth as the morning,
and thine health shall spring forth speedily:
and thy righteousness shall go before thee;
the glory of the Lord shall be thy reward.
Isaiah 58:8

233.

And, behold, there came a leper and worshipped him, saying, Lord, if thou wilt, thou canst make me clean. And Jesus put forth his hand, and touched him, saying, I will; be thou clean. And immediately his leprosy was cleansed.

MATTHEW 8:2–3

234.

Confess your faults one to another, and pray one for another, that ye may be healed.

JAMES 5:16

235.

Bless the LORD, O my soul, and forget not all his benefits: who forgiveth all thine iniquities; who healeth all thy diseases; who redeemeth thy life from destruction; who crowneth thee with lovingkindness and tender mercies.

PSALM 103:2–4

236.

He healeth the broken in heart,
and bindeth up their wounds.

PSALM 147:3

237.

The Spirit of the Lord GOD is upon me;
because the LORD hath anointed me to preach
good tidings unto the meek; he hath sent me
to bind up the brokenhearted, to proclaim
liberty to the captives, and the opening of
the prison to them that are bound.

ISAIAH 61:1

238.

Heal me, O LORD, and I shall be healed; save me,
and I shall be saved: for thou art my praise.

JEREMIAH 17:14

239.

The LORD will strengthen him upon the bed of
languishing: thou wilt make all his bed in his
sickness. I said, LORD, be merciful unto me:
heal my soul; for I have sinned against thee.

PSALM 41:3–4

240.

And when he had called unto him his twelve
disciples, he gave them power against unclean
spirits, to cast them out, and to heal all manner
of sickness and all manner of disease.

MATTHEW 10:1

HEARD

Father, even my closest friends and family sometimes get a glassy, far-off stare when I talk. We're all human, and sometimes we just don't listen to each other. Maybe we're too wrapped up in our own struggles to truly hear and help. I have felt at times that the ceiling was throwing my prayers back at me, but I know that thought is the enemy's attempt to discourage me. My words to You never fall on deaf ears, and they aren't swallowed up in the cacophony of prayers pelting the heavens each day. You will always hear me when I pray, in Jesus' name. Amen.

241.

And this is the confidence that we
have in him, that, if we ask any thing
according to his will, he heareth us.

1 John 5:14

242.

As for me, I will call upon God; and the
Lord shall save me. Evening, and morning,
and at noon, will I pray, and cry aloud:
and he shall hear my voice.

Psalm 55:16–17

243.

Ask, and it shall be given you; seek, and ye shall find; knock, and it shall be opened unto you: for every one that asketh receiveth; and he that seeketh findeth; and to him that knocketh it shall be opened.

MATTHEW 7:7–8

244.

And whatsoever ye shall ask in my name, that will I do, that the Father may be glorified in the Son. If ye shall ask any thing in my name, I will do it.

JOHN 14:13–14

245.

But let him ask in faith, nothing wavering. For he that wavereth is like a wave of the sea driven with the wind and tossed.

JAMES 1:6

246.

Likewise the Spirit also helpeth our infirmities: for we know not what we should pray for as we ought: but the Spirit itself maketh intercession for us with groanings which cannot be uttered.

ROMANS 8:26

247.

The LORD is far from the wicked: but he heareth the prayer of the righteous.

PROVERBS 15:29

248.

But when ye pray, use not vain repetitions, as the heathen do: for they think that they shall be heard for their much speaking. Be not ye therefore like unto them: for your Father knoweth what things ye have need of, before ye ask him.

MATTHEW 6:7–8

249.

For the eyes of the Lord are over the righteous, and his ears are open unto their prayers: but the face of the Lord is against them that do evil.

1 Peter 3:12

250.

The Lord is nigh unto all them that call upon him, to all that call upon him in truth. He will fulfil the desire of them that fear him: he also will hear their cry, and will save them.

Psalm 145:18–19

HELD

Lord, I think of a little child who will climb into her papa's lap just to snuggle—she's content to sit wrapped in the gentle arms of someone who loves her. No matter our age, all people are like that. Sometimes we don't want words or advice or answers—we just need a hug, a connection that communicates love and caring and assures us that things are going to be okay. Thank You, Jesus, that I can run into Your tender and strong arms when I need to be held. I find comfort in the assurance of Your love and compassion, Your strength and control. In Your name I pray, amen.

251.

Blessed be God, even the Father of our Lord Jesus Christ, the Father of mercies, and the God of all comfort; who comforteth us in all our tribulation, that we may be able to comfort them which are in any trouble, by the comfort wherewith we ourselves are comforted of God.

2 Corinthians 1:3–4

252.

Turn thee unto me, and have mercy upon me; for I am desolate and afflicted.

Psalm 25:16

253.

He shall cover thee with his feathers,
and under his wings shalt thou trust:
his truth shall be thy shield and buckler.

PSALM 91:4

254.

Let, I pray thee, thy merciful kindness
be for my comfort, according to
thy word unto thy servant.

PSALM 119:76

255.

Sing, O heavens; and be joyful, O earth;
and break forth into singing, O mountains:
for the LORD hath comforted his people,
and will have mercy upon his afflicted.

ISAIAH 49:13

256.

I, even I, am he that comforteth you: who
art thou, that thou shouldest be afraid of a man
that shall die, and of the son of man which shall
be made as grass; and forgettest the LORD thy
maker, that hath stretched forth the heavens,
and laid the foundations of the earth?

ISAIAH 51:12–13

257.

He shall feed his flock like a shepherd:
he shall gather the lambs with his arm,
and carry them in his bosom.

ISAIAH 40:11

258.

Come unto me, all ye that labour and
are heavy laden, and I will give you rest.

MATTHEW 11:28

259.

And God shall wipe away all tears from their eyes;
and there shall be no more death, neither sorrow,
nor crying, neither shall there be any more pain:
for the former things are passed away.

REVELATION 21:4

———— ∞∞∞ ————

260.

That your sins may be blotted out,
when the times of refreshing shall come
from the presence of the Lord.

ACTS 3:19

HELPED

Father, when children begin to struggle and realize that they need help, they know exactly where to go. They run to their parents with their tears and their aching young frustration, knowing that they won't be turned away. They know that love will compel their mom or dad to hold them, console them, and show them the way through whatever problem they've stumbled over. They rest secure in their parents' guiding hands. But sometimes we adults try to be too self-sufficient. I forget where to turn with my problems. You, Lord, are my help and my salvation. May I never forget to run to You. Amen.

261.

I will lift up mine eyes unto the hills, from
whence cometh my help. My help cometh
from the LORD, which made heaven and earth.

PSALM 121:1–2

262.

Fear thou not; for I am with thee: be not
dismayed; for I am thy God: I will strengthen
thee; yea, I will help thee; yea, I will uphold
thee with the right hand of my righteousness.

ISAIAH 41:10

263.

The LORD taketh my part with them that help me: therefore shall I see my desire upon them that hate me. It is better to trust in the LORD than to put confidence in man.

PSALM 118:7–8

264.

Behold, God is mine helper: the Lord is with them that uphold my soul.

PSALM 54:4

265.

And I will pray the Father, and he shall give you another Comforter, that he may abide with you for ever.

JOHN 14:16

266.
But I am poor and needy; yet the Lord thinketh
upon me: thou art my help and my deliverer;
make no tarrying, O my God.

PSALM 40:17

267.
But the Comforter, which is the Holy Ghost,
whom the Father will send in my name, he shall
teach you all things, and bring all things to your
remembrance, whatsoever I have said unto you.

JOHN 14:26

268.
Hear, O LORD, and have mercy upon me:
LORD, be thou my helper.

PSALM 30:10

269.

For the Lord GOD will help me;
therefore shall I not be confounded:
therefore have I set my face like a flint,
and I know that I shall not be ashamed.

ISAIAH 50:7

270.

Let us therefore come boldly unto the throne
of grace, that we may obtain mercy, and
find grace to help in time of need.

HEBREWS 4:16

IMPROVED

Lord, we all have those friends who make us better for having spent time with them. They're encouraging and caring, but honest. They push us to be the best version of ourselves. Jesus, I am better when I'm with You. You lovingly convict me of my errors and lift me up out of my discouragement. You know everything there is to know about me—You've seen the best of me and the worst—and yet You still love me. Living Your way has brought joy and peace into my days. Keep working on me! In the name of Jesus I pray, amen.

271.

Wherefore lay apart all filthiness and superfluity of naughtiness, and receive with meekness the engrafted word, which is able to save your souls.

JAMES 1:21

272.

All scripture is given by inspiration of God, and is profitable for doctrine, for reproof, for correction, for instruction in righteousness: that the man of God may be perfect, thoroughly furnished unto all good works.

2 TIMOTHY 3:16–17

273.

But the fruit of the Spirit is love, joy, peace,
longsuffering, gentleness, goodness, faith,
meekness, temperance: against such there
is no law. And they that are Christ's have
crucified the flesh with the affections and lusts

GALATIANS 5:22–24

274.

And such were some of you: but ye are
washed, but ye are sanctified, but ye are
justified in the name of the Lord Jesus,
and by the Spirit of our God.

1 CORINTHIANS 6:11

275.

Pure religion and undefiled before God
and the Father is this, To visit the fatherless
and widows in their affliction, and to keep
himself unspotted from the world.

JAMES 1:27

276.

Ye have put off the old man with his deeds;
and have put on the new man, which is
renewed in knowledge after the image
of him that created him.

COLOSSIANS 3:9–10

277.

If so be that ye have heard him, and have been
taught by him, as the truth is in Jesus: that ye put
off concerning the former conversation the old
man, which is corrupt according to the deceitful
lusts; and be renewed in the spirit of your mind.

EPHESIANS 4:21–23

278.

Therefore if any man be in Christ,
he is a new creature: old things are passed
away; behold, all things are become new.

2 CORINTHIANS 5:17

279.

Whatsoever things are true, whatsoever things are honest, whatsoever things are just, whatsoever things are pure, whatsoever things are lovely, whatsoever things are of good report; if there be any virtue, and if there be any praise, think on these things.

PHILIPPIANS 4:8

280.

This is my commandment, That ye love one another, as I have loved you.

JOHN 15:12

JUSTIFIED

*God, new-fallen snow is like a fresh beginning. It
blankets the ground and makes everything new. It
covers all the ugliness with sparkling, white purity.
Just like Jesus does for us. We borrow His righteousness
and are clothed in shining white robes, not because
we are that good or because we've earned them, but
because He died to scour us clean of all our spots and
blemishes. When I meet You face-to-face, Jesus, I'm
covered in garments of grace and all my stains are
washed by Your blood. You won't see the old me, the
wretched, dirty beggar. You'll see Your child. Amen.*

281.

And such were some of you: but ye are
washed, but ye are sanctified, but ye are
justified in the name of the Lord Jesus,
and by the Spirit of our God.

1 CORINTHIANS 6:11

282.

For by grace are ye saved through faith; and that
not of yourselves: it is the gift of God: not of
works, lest any man should boast.

EPHESIANS 2:8–9

283.

Who gave himself for our sins, that he might deliver us from this present evil world, according to the will of God and our Father.

GALATIANS 1:4

284.

For whom he did foreknow, he also did predestinate to be conformed to the image of his Son, that he might be the firstborn among many brethren. Moreover whom he did predestinate, them he also called: and whom he called, them he also justified: and whom he justified, them he also glorified.

ROMANS 8:29–30

285.

Therefore being justified by faith, we have peace with God through our Lord Jesus Christ.

ROMANS 5:1

286.

But to him that worketh not, but believeth
on him that justifieth the ungodly,
his faith is counted for righteousness.

ROMANS 4:5

287.

Knowing that a man is not justified by the
works of the law, but by the faith of Jesus Christ,
even we have believed in Jesus Christ, that we
might be justified by the faith of Christ, and not
by the works of the law: for by the works of
the law shall no flesh be justified.

GALATIANS 2:16

288.

And he believed in the LORD; and he
counted it to him for righteousness.

GENESIS 15:6

289.

Wherefore the law was our schoolmaster to bring us unto Christ, that we might be justified by faith.

GALATIANS 3:24

290.

If thou shalt confess with thy mouth the Lord Jesus, and shalt believe in thine heart that God hath raised him from the dead, thou shalt be saved. For with the heart man believeth unto righteousness; and with the mouth confession is made unto salvation.

ROMANS 10:9–10

KEPT

God, I am Yours. Satan whispers nasty lies about who I am—he says that I'm dirty, unworthy, unwanted—but I know the truth. I know that I belong to You. And nothing can separate me from Your love. No one can snatch me from Your hand! You love me extravagantly and tenderly care for all of my needs—both spiritual and physical. You have seen all the days of my life and planned out every step of my journey. No matter what hardships I face in this life, no matter what fears assault me, I rest safely in the palm of Your hand. Amen.

291.

And I give unto them eternal life; and they shall never perish, neither shall any man pluck them out of my hand. My Father, which gave them me, is greater than all; and no man is able to pluck them out of my Father's hand.

JOHN 10:28–29

292.

Keep me as the apple of the eye,
hide me under the shadow of thy wings.

PSALM 17:8

293.

For ye are dead, and your life is hid with Christ
in God. When Christ, who is our life, shall
appear, then shall ye also appear with him in glory.

COLOSSIANS 3:3–4

294.

Then we which are alive and remain shall
be caught up together with them in the
clouds, to meet the Lord in the air: and
so shall we ever be with the Lord.

1 THESSALONIANS 4:17

295.

For God so loved the world, that he gave his only
begotten Son, that whosoever believeth in him
should not perish, but have everlasting life.

JOHN 3:16

296.
Are not five sparrows sold for two farthings,
and not one of them is forgotten before God?
LUKE 12:6

297.
Wherefore, if God so clothe the grass of
the field, which to day is, and to morrow
is cast into the oven, shall he not much
more clothe you, O ye of little faith?
MATTHEW 6:30

298.
He shall cover thee with his feathers,
and under his wings shalt thou trust:
his truth shall be thy shield and buckler.
PSALM 91:4

299.
Behold, he that keepeth Israel shall neither
slumber nor sleep. The LORD is thy keeper:
the LORD is thy shade upon thy right hand.
PSALM 121:4–5

300.
The name of the LORD is a strong tower:
the righteous runneth into it, and is safe.
PROVERBS 18:10

KNOWN

Lord, we humans all search for someone who understands us. We want to be known. And not only do we want to be known, but we want to be accepted and loved for who we are—in spite of our flaws and foibles. You are that Friend, Jesus. You love me with perfect love and You know me completely. You made me to be just who I am. You've searched the deepest reaches of my soul. You've celebrated my best and mourned my worst with me. And You've never left me. You understand me, as the Potter who contours my clay into something of beauty. Amen.

301.
Thou hast searched me, and known me.
Thou knowest my downsitting and mine
uprising, thou understandest my thought afar off.

PSALM 139:1–2

302.
Thine eyes did see my substance, yet being
unperfect; and in thy book all my members
were written, which in continuance were fashioned, when as yet there was none of them.

PSALM 139:16

303.

But thou, O LORD, knowest me: thou hast seen
me, and tried mine heart toward thee.

JEREMIAH 12:3

304.

Before I formed thee in the belly I knew thee.

JEREMIAH 1:5

305.

The LORD seeth not as man seeth; for man
looketh on the outward appearance,
but the LORD looketh on the heart.

1 SAMUEL 16:7

306.

Neither is there any creature that is
not manifest in his sight: but all things
are naked and opened unto the eyes
of him with whom we have to do.

HEBREWS 4:13

307.

But the very hairs of your
head are all numbered.

MATTHEW 10:30

308.

For his eyes are upon the ways of man,
and he seeth all his goings.

JOB 34:21

309.
The LORD looketh from heaven; he beholdeth
all the sons of men. From the place of his
habitation he looketh upon all the inhabitants
of the earth. He fashioneth their hearts alike;
he considereth all their works.

PSALM 33:13–15

⸺∘∞∘⸺

310.
Your Father knoweth what things
ye have need of, before ye ask him.

MATTHEW 6:8

LONGED FOR

God, I'm stunned to realize that You, the God of the universe, want to know me and be known by me. It's astonishing that You miss me when I'm far from You and long for me just as parents long to see their children's happy grins and hear their chatter when they've been away. You want a relationship with me— little, insignificant me. But to You I'm not a nobody. I'm Your precious, beloved child! You are the Potter who formed me inside and out, and You know me more intimately than any other. I want to live my entire life with You. Amen.

311.

I am sought of them that asked not for me;
I am found of them that sought me not: I said,
Behold me, behold me, unto a nation that was
not called by my name. I have spread out my
hands all the day unto a rebellious people.

ISAIAH 65:1–2

312.

Behold, I stand at the door, and knock:
if any man hear my voice, and open
the door, I will come in to him,
and will sup with him, and he with me.

REVELATION 3:20

313.

Draw nigh to God,
and he will draw nigh to you.

JAMES 4:8

314.

What man of you, having an hundred sheep,
if he lose one of them, doth not leave the
ninety and nine in the wilderness, and go
after that which is lost, until he find it?

LUKE 15:4

315.

How often would I have gathered thy children
together, even as a hen gathereth her chickens
under her wings, and ye would not!

MATTHEW 23:37

316.

And therefore will the Lord wait, that he may
be gracious unto you, and therefore will he be
exalted, that he may have mercy upon you.

ISAIAH 30:18

317.

But as many as received him, to them gave
he power to become the sons of God,
even to them that believe on his name.

JOHN 1:12

318.

The Lord is not slack concerning his promise,
as some men count slackness; but is longsuffering
to us-ward, not willing that any should perish,
but that all should come to repentance.

2 PETER 3:9

319.

For this is good and acceptable in the sight of God our Saviour; who will have all men to be saved, and to come unto the knowledge of the truth.

1 Timothy 2:3–4

320.

And I will walk among you, and will be your God, and ye shall be my people.

Leviticus 26:12

LOVED

God, You are infinitely far above me. I wonder how You could love me, but You do. And I know Your love isn't just a feeling or whim—it is the very fiber of Your being. Love is who You are. You can't do anything other than love me because You are love, Lord. And You command me to love as You do—sacrificially and freely. Jesus, You gave up glory to prove Your great love for me. You died in my place. Your love humbles and amazes me. May Your Spirit give me strength to love until it hurts. Amen.

321.

For God so loved the world, that he gave his only begotten Son, that whosoever believeth in him should not perish, but have everlasting life.

JOHN 3:16

322.

God is love. In this was manifested the love of God toward us, because that God sent his only begotten Son into the world, that we might live through him.

1 JOHN 4:8–9

323.

For I am persuaded, that neither death,
nor life, nor angels, nor principalities,
nor powers, nor things present, nor things
to come, nor height, nor depth, nor any other
creature, shall be able to separate us from the
love of God, which is in Christ Jesus our Lord.

ROMANS 8:38–39

324.

But God commendeth his love toward us, in that,
while we were yet sinners, Christ died for us.

ROMANS 5:8

325.

And we have known and believed the love that
God hath to us. God is love; and he that dwelleth
in love dwelleth in God, and God in him.

1 JOHN 4:16

326.

The LORD hath appeared of old unto me, saying,
Yea, I have loved thee with an everlasting love:
therefore with lovingkindness have I drawn thee.

JEREMIAH 31:3

327.

But God, who is rich in mercy, for his great
love wherewith he loved us, even when we
were dead in sins, hath quickened us together
with Christ, (by grace ye are saved;) and hath
raised us up together, and made us sit together
in heavenly places in Christ Jesus.

EPHESIANS 2:4–6

328.

This is my commandment, That ye love
one another, as I have loved you.

JOHN 15:12

329.

Because thy lovingkindness is better
than life, my lips shall praise thee.

PSALM 63:3

———∞∞∞———

330.

For the Father himself loveth you.

JOHN 16:27

NAMED

Father in heaven, the enemy whispers lies into my ear.
He tries to defeat me by saying that I'm unworthy,
unwanted, unloved, forgotten. He tells me that I'm
nothing. He tells me that I'm hopeless. But I choose to
ignore his poisonous murmurs. I choose to listen to Your
Word. And You have given me a new name. You say I'm
cherished. Loved. Known. Forgiven. Accepted. You say
I'm Yours. And to the victorious You promise a white
stone with a new name written on it. God, give me the
victory today because I want to hold a white stone at
Your return. In Jesus' name, amen.

331.

To him that overcometh will I give to eat of the
hidden manna, and will give him a white stone,
and in the stone a new name written, which no
man knoweth saving he that receiveth it.

REVELATION 2:17

332.

And ye shall leave your name for a curse unto
my chosen: for the Lord GOD shall slay thee,
and call his servants by another name.

ISAIAH 65:15

333.

Even unto them will I give in mine house and within my walls a place and a name better than of sons and of daughters: I will give them an everlasting name, that shall not be cut off.

Isaiah 56:5

334.

And the Gentiles shall see thy righteousness, and all kings thy glory: and thou shalt be called by a new name, which the mouth of the Lord shall name.

Isaiah 62:2

335.

But now thus saith the Lord that created thee, O Jacob, and he that formed thee, O Israel, Fear not: for I have redeemed thee, I have called thee by thy name; thou art mine.

Isaiah 43:1

336.

But as many as received him, to them gave
he power to become the sons of God,
even to them that believe on his name.

JOHN 1:12

337.

Him that overcometh will I make a pillar
in the temple of my God, and he shall go no
more out: and I will write upon him the name
of my God, and the name of the city of my
God, which is new Jerusalem, which cometh
down out of heaven from my God: and I
will write upon him my new name.

REVELATION 3:12

338.

Therefore if any man be in Christ, he is a
new creature: old things are passed away;
behold, all things are become new.

2 CORINTHIANS 5:17

339.

As for me, behold, my covenant is with thee,
and thou shalt be a father of many nations.
Neither shall thy name any more be called
Abram, but thy name shall be Abraham; for a
father of many nations have I made thee.

GENESIS 17:4–5

340.

I will have mercy upon her that had not
obtained mercy; and I will say to them which
were not my people, Thou art my people;
and they shall say, Thou art my God.

HOSEA 2:23

PARDONED

*God, I can hardly believe it! I thought that my
sentence was irreversible. I've sinned. I've messed up.
My punishment was not misplaced. I wasn't wrongly
accused—I'm guilty of every wrong deed placed on
my account and I deserved Your condemnation. But
then a miraculous thing happened. Instead of serving
an eternal sentence, locked away from You for all time,
I received a pardon. I'm free. My debt was paid by
You. Thank You, Jesus! Amen.*

341.
For the wages of sin is death; but the gift of God
is eternal life through Jesus Christ our Lord.
ROMANS 6:23

342.
That if thou shalt confess with thy mouth
the Lord Jesus, and shalt believe in thine
heart that God hath raised him from the dead,
thou shalt be saved. For with the heart man
believeth unto righteousness; and with the
mouth confession is made unto salvation.
ROMANS 10:9–10

343.

My little children, these things write I unto
you, that ye sin not. And if any man sin,
we have an advocate with the Father, Jesus
Christ the righteous: and he is the propitiation
for our sins: and not for ours only, but also
for the sins of the whole world.

1 JOHN 2:1–2

———— ∞ ————

344.

For by grace are ye saved through faith;
and that not of yourselves: it is the gift of God.

EPHESIANS 2:8

———— ∞ ————

345.

As far as the east is from the west, so far
hath he removed our transgressions from us.

PSALM 103:12

346.

For thou, Lord, art good, and ready
to forgive; and plenteous in mercy
unto all them that call upon thee.

PSALM 86:5

347.

He will turn again, he will have compassion upon
us; he will subdue our iniquities; and thou wilt
cast all their sins into the depths of the sea.

MICAH 7:19

348.

Verily, verily, I say unto you, He that heareth
my word, and believeth on him that sent me,
hath everlasting life, and shall not come into
condemnation; but is passed from death unto life.

JOHN 5:24

349.

To wit, that God was in Christ, reconciling the world unto himself, not imputing their trespasses unto them; and hath committed unto us the word of reconciliation.

2 CORINTHIANS 5:19

350.

For this is my blood of the new testament, which is shed for many for the remission of sins.

MATTHEW 26:28

PERFECTED

Father, please soften the dried clay of my heart so that it yields to Your sculpting hand. Help me to heed Your Holy Spirit's urgings. You are the Master Artist who would mold my heart into a thing of beauty if I surrender my will to Yours. I'm so grateful that You don't give up on me. Even when I falter and stray from You, You're capable of redeeming my mistakes and making me more like Jesus. Continue to rework my heart until I reach perfection in Your presence. In Jesus' name, amen.

351.

For our conversation is in heaven; from whence also we look for the Saviour, the Lord Jesus Christ: who shall change our vile body, that it may be fashioned like unto his glorious body, according to the working whereby he is able even to subdue all things unto himself.

PHILIPPIANS 3:20–21

352.

Being confident of this very thing, that he which hath begun a good work in you will perform it until the day of Jesus Christ.

PHILIPPIANS 1:6

353.

But whoso keepeth his word, in him
verily is the love of God perfected:
hereby know we that we are in him.

1 John 2:5

354.

For we know that if our earthly house of
this tabernacle were dissolved, we have
a building of God, an house not made
with hands, eternal in the heavens.

2 Corinthians 5:1

355.

But now being made free from sin, and
become servants to God, ye have your fruit
unto holiness, and the end everlasting life.

Romans 6:22

356.

This I say then, Walk in the Spirit,
and ye shall not fulfil the lust of the flesh.

GALATIANS 5:16

357.

In a moment, in the twinkling of an eye,
at the last trump: for the trumpet shall
sound, and the dead shall be raised
incorruptible, and we shall be changed.
For this corruptible must put on incorruption,
and this mortal must put on immortality.

1 CORINTHIANS 15:52–53

358.

So also is the resurrection of the dead. It is
sown in corruption; it is raised in incorruption.

1 CORINTHIANS 15:42

359.

Beloved, now are we the sons of God, and it doth not yet appear what we shall be: but we know that, when he shall appear, we shall be like him; for we shall see him as he is. And every man that hath this hope in him purifieth himself, even as he is pure.

1 John 3:2–3

360.

For I delight in the law of God after the inward man.

Romans 7:22

PREPARED

*Lord, when You call me to do something for Your
kingdom, You don't leave me to figure it out on my own.
When You call, You equip, You enable, You provide.
You outfit me specifically for the task You've called me
to do. You give me the strength and the ability for the
work ahead. You already know what skills I'll need for
the specific tasks you've selected in advance for me to
do. Help me to trust Your preparations and to actively
ready myself to be an effective tool in Your hand. In
Jesus' name, amen.*

361.
For we are his workmanship, created in Christ
Jesus unto good works, which God hath before
ordained that we should walk in them.

EPHESIANS 2:10

362.
Moreover whom he did predestinate, them he
also called: and whom he called, them he also
justified: and whom he justified, them he also
glorified. What shall we then say to these things?
If God be for us, who can be against us?

ROMANS 8:30–31

363.

Now the God of peace, that brought again from the dead our Lord Jesus. . .make you perfect in every good work to do his will, working in you that which is wellpleasing in his sight, through Jesus Christ; to whom be glory for ever and ever.

HEBREWS 13:20–21

364.

Also I heard the voice of the Lord, saying, Whom shall I send, and who will go for us? Then said I, Here am I; send me.

ISAIAH 6:8

365.

For if thou altogether holdest thy peace at this time, then shall there enlargement and deliverance arise to the Jews from another place; but thou and thy father's house shall be destroyed: and who knoweth whether thou art come to the kingdom for such a time as this?

ESTHER 4:14

366.

For I know the thoughts that I think
toward you, saith the LORD, thoughts of peace,
and not of evil, to give you an expected end.

JEREMIAH 29:11

367.

For it is God which worketh in you both
to will and to do of his good pleasure.

PHILIPPIANS 2:13

368.

David said moreover, The LORD that delivered
me out of the paw of the lion, and out of the
paw of the bear, he will deliver me out of the
hand of this Philistine. And Saul said unto
David, Go, and the LORD be with thee.

1 SAMUEL 17:37

369.

And the LORD said unto Moses, See, I have
made thee a god to Pharaoh: and Aaron thy
brother shall be thy prophet. Thou shalt speak
all that I command thee: and Aaron thy brother
shall speak unto Pharaoh, that he send the
children of Israel out of his land.

EXODUS 7:1–2

———⚬⚬⚬———

370.

Behold, I am the LORD, the God of all flesh:
is there any thing too hard for me?

JEREMIAH 32:27

PROTECTED

*Father, I've entertained the wrong image of You. I had
thought that You condemned me, that I had to be perfect
in order to be accepted by You. But I don't have to put
on my Sunday clothes for You. You don't look on me
with censure and anger and impatience as I stumble
along after You—You see me with eyes of compassion.
You know that I'm harassed and helpless, a lamb in
need of a strong and caring shepherd. Thank You, Jesus,
for Your compassionate care and protection. In Your
name I pray, amen.*

371.

When he saw the multitudes, he was moved
with compassion on them, because they
fainted, and were scattered abroad,
as sheep having no shepherd.

MATTHEW 9:36

372.

Be strong and of a good courage, fear not,
nor be afraid of them: for the LORD thy
God, he it is that doth go with thee;
he will not fail thee, nor forsake thee.

DEUTERONOMY 31:6

373.

Speak to the earth, and it shall teach thee: and the fishes of the sea shall declare unto thee. Who knoweth not in all these that the hand of the Lord hath wrought this? In whose hand is the soul of every living thing, and the breath of all mankind.

Job 12:8–10

374.

But the Lord is faithful, who shall stablish you, and keep you from evil.

2 Thessalonians 3:3

375.

But let all those that put their trust in thee rejoice: let them ever shout for joy, because thou defendest them: let them also that love thy name be joyful in thee.

Psalm 5:11

376.

God is our refuge and strength,
a very present help in trouble.

PSALM 46:1

377.

LORD, thou hast heard the desire of the
humble: thou wilt prepare their heart,
thou wilt cause thine ear to hear: to judge
the fatherless and the oppressed, that the
man of the earth may no more oppress.

PSALM 10:17–18

378.

Though I walk in the midst of trouble,
thou wilt revive me: thou shalt stretch
forth thine hand against the wrath of mine
enemies, and thy right hand shall save me.

PSALM 138:7

379.

We are troubled on every side, yet not distressed;
we are perplexed, but not in despair; persecuted,
but not forsaken; cast down, but not destroyed.

2 CORINTHIANS 4:8–9

380.

He shall cover thee with his feathers,
and under his wings shalt thou trust:
his truth shall be thy shield and buckler.
Thou shalt not be afraid for the terror by
night; nor for the arrow that flieth by day.

PSALM 91:4–5

PROVIDED FOR

Lord, Your goodness flows to those who look for and depend on You. In my stubbornness, I try to do things my own way, believing I am self-reliant. I quote Your Word as "I can do all things," too often forgetting the "through Christ who strengthens me" part. I think that I should be my own answer and create my own solutions. But when the plates I'm spinning fall and shatter at my feet, I remember to seek You, Lord. You are my provision, so I wait for You. In Jesus' name, amen.

381.

The Lord is good unto them that wait for him,
to the soul that seeketh him. It is good that
a man should both hope and quietly
wait for the salvation of the Lord.
LAMENTATIONS 3:25–26

382.

Therefore take no thought, saying, What shall
we eat? or, What shall we drink? or, Wherewithal
shall we be clothed? (For after all these things
do the Gentiles seek:) for your heavenly Father
knoweth that ye have need of all these things.
MATTHEW 6:31–32

383.

But my God shall supply all your need according to his riches in glory by Christ Jesus.

PHILIPPIANS 4:19

384.

Consider the ravens: for they neither sow nor reap; which neither have storehouse nor barn; and God feedeth them: how much more are ye better than the fowls?

LUKE 12:24

385.

From whence come wars and fightings among you? come they not hence, even of your lusts that war in your members? Ye lust, and have not: ye kill, and desire to have, and cannot obtain: ye fight and war, yet ye have not, because ye ask not.

JAMES 4:1–2

386.

Who provideth for the raven his food?
when his young ones cry unto God,
they wander for lack of meat.

Job 38:41

387.

There hath no temptation taken you but such as
is common to man: but God is faithful, who will
not suffer you to be tempted above that ye are
able; but will with the temptation also make a
way to escape, that ye may be able to bear it.

1 Corinthians 10:13

388.

And God is able to make all grace abound toward
you; that ye, always having all sufficiency in all
things, may abound to every good work.

2 Corinthians 9:8

389.

The eyes of all wait upon thee; and thou
givest them their meat in due season.
Thou openest thine hand, and satisfiest
the desire of every living thing.

PSALM 145:15–16

―――⊶⊷―――

390.

For the LORD God is a sun and shield: the LORD
will give grace and glory: no good thing will
he withhold from them that walk uprightly.

PSALM 84:11

QUICKENED

Father, in the story of Pinocchio, *a wooden puppet wanted to become a real boy. I too desire real life. I want a living heart that's tender and responsive to Your urgings. Take away the hardness of my stubborn pride. I can't give myself a new heart, Lord, but You are the great Quickener. Without You I'm just a puppet to the world's pleasures, but Your Spirit can cut my strings and give me new life. I want to truly live! In Jesus' name, amen.*

391.

A new heart also will I give you, and a new
spirit will I put within you: and I will take
away the stony heart out of your flesh,
and I will give you an heart of flesh.

EZEKIEL 36:26

392.

I am crucified with Christ: nevertheless I
live; yet not I, but Christ liveth in me:
and the life which I now live in the flesh I
live by the faith of the Son of God, who
loved me, and gave himself for me.

GALATIANS 2:20

393.

And you hath he quickened, who
were dead in trespasses and sins.

EPHESIANS 2:1

394.

Even when we were dead in sins, hath quickened
us together with Christ, (by grace ye are saved;)
and hath raised us up together, and made us sit
together in heavenly places in Christ Jesus.

EPHESIANS 2:5–6

395.

Hide thy face from my sins, and blot out all
mine iniquities. Create in me a clean heart,
O God; and renew a right spirit within me.

PSALM 51:9–10

396.

Not by works of righteousness which we have done, but according to his mercy he saved us, by the washing of regeneration, and renewing of the Holy Ghost.

TITUS 3:5

397.

For to be carnally minded is death; but to be spiritually minded is life and peace.

ROMANS 8:6

398.

For in him we live, and move, and have our being; as certain also of your own poets have said, For we are also his offspring.

ACTS 17:28

399.

For as in Adam all die, even so
in Christ shall all be made alive.

1 CORINTHIANS 15:22

400.

Neither yield ye your members as
instruments of unrighteousness unto sin:
but yield yourselves unto God, as those that
are alive from the dead, and your members
as instruments of righteousness unto God.

ROMANS 6:13

RECONCILED

*God, I'm broken. I live in a broken world, enmeshed
in an existence filled with war and hatred, selfishness
and abuse. I've run after success and relationships, but
I can't mend what's wrong by using the things of this
world. I can't fix the sin in my life—but You can, Jesus.
God, all I have to do is surrender to You and repent.
You came and died so that I could be regenerated into
something new in Christ. I'm not broken anymore! I
have been remade in Jesus, reconciled to God. I am new!
Thank You, and amen.*

401.

And all things are of God, who hath reconciled
us to himself by Jesus Christ, and hath
given to us the ministry of reconciliation.

2 CORINTHIANS 5:18

402.

For if, when we were enemies, we were reconciled to God by the death of his Son, much more,
being reconciled, we shall be saved by his life.

ROMANS 5:10

403.

Therefore being justified by faith, we have peace
with God through our Lord Jesus Christ.

ROMANS 5:1

404.

Blessed be the God and Father of our Lord Jesus
Christ. . .according as he hath chosen us in him
before the foundation of the world, that we should
be holy and without blame before him in love.

EPHESIANS 1:3–4

405.

Now then we are ambassadors for Christ,
as though God did beseech you by us: we pray
you in Christ's stead, be ye reconciled to God.

2 CORINTHIANS 5:20

406.

And, having made peace through the blood of
his cross, by him to reconcile all things unto
himself; by him, I say, whether they be things in
earth, or things in heaven. And you, that were
sometime alienated and enemies in your mind
by wicked works, yet now hath he reconciled.

COLOSSIANS 1:20–21

407.

Repent ye therefore, and be converted,
that your sins may be blotted out.

Acts 3:19

408.

He that believeth on the Son hath everlasting life:
and he that believeth not the Son shall not see
life; but the wrath of God abideth on him.

JOHN 3:36

409.

For if the casting away of them be the
reconciling of the world, what shall the
receiving of them be, but life from the dead?

ROMANS 11:15

410.

And that he might reconcile both
unto God in one body by the cross,
having slain the enmity thereby.

EPHESIANS 2:16

REDEEMED

Father, the habits of sin are difficult to break. I think I'm maturing, but suddenly I'm blindsided by another misstep. I repeat a cycle of sin I thought I'd left behind. I fear I've disappointed You as I fall hard on my face. But then I look up and see Your nail-pierced hand held out to me. You have redeemed me from that empty way of life. You died for me, providing an unblemished sacrifice to purchase my freedom. Even when I falter I'm no longer enslaved by my old attitudes and actions—because I've been redeemed. I'm bought by Your blood and I belong to You. Amen.

411.

Forasmuch as ye know that ye were not redeemed with corruptible things, as silver and gold, from your vain conversation received by tradition from your fathers; but with the precious blood of Christ, as of a lamb without blemish and without spot.

1 PETER 1:18–19

412.

Fear not: for I have redeemed thee, I have called thee by thy name; thou art mine.

ISAIAH 43:1

413.

For God sent not his Son into the world
to condemn the world; but that the
world through him might be saved.

JOHN 3:17

414.

For the wages of sin is death; but the gift of God
is eternal life through Jesus Christ our Lord.

ROMANS 6:23

415.

And they sung a new song, saying, Thou art
worthy to take the book, and to open the seals
thereof: for thou wast slain, and hast redeemed
us to God by thy blood out of every kindred,
and tongue, and people, and nation.

REVELATION 5:9

416.

Know ye not that your body is the temple of the
Holy Ghost which is in you, which ye have of
God, and ye are not your own? For ye are bought
with a price: therefore glorify God in your body,
and in your spirit, which are God's.

1 CORINTHIANS 6:19–20

417.

But when the fulness of the time was come, God
sent forth his Son, made of a woman, made under
the law, to redeem them that were under the law,
that we might receive the adoption of sons.

GALATIANS 4:4–5

418.

I will ransom them from the power of the grave;
I will redeem them from death: O death, I will be
thy plagues; O grave, I will be thy destruction.

HOSEA 13:14

419.

The Spirit of the Lord is upon me,
because he hath anointed me to preach the
gospel to the poor; he hath sent me to heal
the brokenhearted, to preach deliverance to
the captives, and recovering of sight to the
blind, to set at liberty them that are bruised.

Luke 4:18

420.

But he was wounded for our transgressions,
he was bruised for our iniquities:
the chastisement of our peace was upon
him; and with his stripes we are healed.

Isaiah 53:5

REFRESHED

*Lord, I was tired, worn out, and beaten down—
exhausted from fighting the same old battles every day.
I was emotionally on edge and about to graduate to hot
mess. But You give strength to the weary and rest to the
burdened. Instead of losing patience with me, You lovingly
lead me to the rest and restoration that I crave. You restore
me to strength and refresh my perspective. Thank You for
providing for all my needs—both physical and spiritual.
Please show me how to deal kindly with others when they
need refreshment. In the name of Jesus I pray, amen.*

421.

The LORD is my shepherd; I shall not want.
He maketh me to lie down in green pastures:
he leadeth me beside the still waters. He
restoreth my soul: he leadeth me in the paths
of righteousness for his name's sake.

PSALM 23:1–3

422.

Repent ye therefore, and be converted, that
your sins may be blotted out, when the times of
refreshing shall come from the presence of the Lord.

ACTS 3:19

423.

The law of the LORD is perfect, converting
the soul: the testimony of the LORD
is sure, making wise the simple.

PSALM 19:7

424.

Thou, O God, didst send a plentiful
rain, whereby thou didst confirm thine
inheritance, when it was weary.

PSALM 68:9

425.

For I have satiated the weary soul, and I
have replenished every sorrowful soul.

JEREMIAH 31:25

426.

That I may come unto you with joy by the
will of God, and may with you be refreshed.

ROMANS 15:32

427.

For they have refreshed my spirit and yours:
therefore acknowledge ye them that are such.

1 CORINTHIANS 16:18

428.

Therefore we were comforted in your
comfort: yea, and exceedingly the more
joyed we for the joy of Titus, because
his spirit was refreshed by you all.

2 CORINTHIANS 7:13

429.

For we have great joy and consolation
in thy love, because the bowels of the
saints are refreshed by thee, brother.

Philemon 7

430.

But they that wait upon the Lord shall renew
their strength; they shall mount up with wings
as eagles; they shall run, and not be weary;
and they shall walk, and not faint.

Isaiah 40:31

RENEWED

God, our perspective can carve us like a sculptor's chisel. I often fixate on my problems and failures. Compared to the comfort and ease of some in this world, the believer's journey can seem rigorous and far too challenging. When I focus on the here and now, discouragement edges into my thoughts—because I've lost sight of the kingdom I'm waiting for. But, Lord, You call this life a passing discomfort that will earn me eternal glory! Keep my mind from straying to the temporary. Then I will live for You, undaunted by my earthly circumstances, and I will be inwardly renewed every day. Amen.

431.

For which cause we faint not; but though our outward man perish, yet the inward man is renewed day by day. For our light affliction, which is but for a moment, worketh for us a far more exceeding and eternal weight of glory.

2 CORINTHIANS 4:16–17

432.

Create in me a clean heart, O God; and renew a right spirit within me.

PSALM 51:10

433.

And be not conformed to this world: but be
ye transformed by the renewing of your
mind, that ye may prove what is that good,
and acceptable, and perfect, will of God.

ROMANS 12:2

434.

Ye have put off the old man with his deeds; and
have put on the new man, which is renewed in
knowledge after the image of him that created him.

COLOSSIANS 3:9–10

435.

Not by works of righteousness which we
have done, but according to his mercy he
saved us, by the washing of regeneration,
and renewing of the Holy Ghost.

TITUS 3:5

436.

Then shall the lame man leap as an hart, and the
tongue of the dumb sing: for in the wilderness
shall waters break out, and streams in the desert.

Isaiah 35:6

437.

I will open rivers in high places,
and fountains in the midst of the valleys:
I will make the wilderness a pool of water,
and the dry land springs of water.

Isaiah 41:18

438.

And God shall wipe away all tears from their
eyes; and there shall be no more death, neither
sorrow, nor crying, neither shall there be any
more pain: for the former things are passed
away. And he that sat upon the throne said,
Behold, I make all things new.

Revelation 21:4–5

439.

That ye put off concerning the former
conversation the old man, which is corrupt
according to the deceitful lusts; and be
renewed in the spirit of your mind; and that
ye put on the new man, which after God is
created in righteousness and true holiness.

EPHESIANS 4:22–24

440.

Let us draw near with a true heart in
full assurance of faith, having our hearts
sprinkled from an evil conscience,
and our bodies washed with pure water.

HEBREWS 10:22

SATISFIED

Father, I have eaten my fill only to hear my stomach grumbling for more in a few short hours. My physical body burns through food and craves more—always more. Spiritually I have the same insatiable appetite. I've tried to satisfy it with the junk food of society. I've consumed the world's buffet of living for myself, but after a while I feel empty again. However, Jesus, You are the bread of life, living sustenance that fills my void and never leaves me hungry. In You I have found what my soul craves. In Jesus' name, amen.

441.

And Jesus said unto them, I am the bread of life: he that cometh to me shall never hunger; and he that believeth on me shall never thirst.

JOHN 6:35

442.

Jesus answered and said unto her, Whosoever drinketh of this water shall thirst again: but whosoever drinketh of the water that I shall give him shall never thirst; but the water that I shall give him shall be in him a well of water springing up into everlasting life.

JOHN 4:13–14

443.

Blessed are they which do hunger and thirst after righteousness: for they shall be filled.

MATTHEW 5:6

444.

O God, thou art my God; early will I seek thee: my soul thirsteth for thee, my flesh longeth for thee in a dry and thirsty land, where no water is; to see thy power and thy glory, so as I have seen thee in the sanctuary.

PSALM 63:1–2

445.

For I have satiated the weary soul, and I have replenished every sorrowful soul.

JEREMIAH 31:25

446.

The people asked, and he brought quails,
and satisfied them with the bread of heaven.
He opened the rock, and the waters gushed
out; they ran in the dry places like a river.

PSALM 105:40–41

447.

The meek shall eat and be satisfied:
they shall praise the LORD that seek him:
your heart shall live for ever.

PSALM 22:26

448.

O satisfy us early with thy mercy; that we
may rejoice and be glad all our days.

PSALM 90:14

449.

Ho, every one that thirsteth, come ye to the
waters, and he that hath no money; come ye,
buy, and eat; yea, come, buy wine and milk
without money and without price. Wherefore
do ye spend money for that which is not bread?
and your labour for that which satisfieth not?

Isaiah 55:1–2

450.

Thou openest thine hand, and satisfiest
the desire of every living thing.

Psalm 145:16

SAVED

*God, I'm so grateful that I can be confident in my
salvation. I don't have to wonder if there's a scale
weighing my deeds, or if it will tip in favor of goodness.
That's because You did all the work, Jesus! I will live
forever with You because Your blood covers my sin.
The enemy may try to convince me that what I've done
has crossed the borders of Your grace, but I know the
truth of Your limitless mercy. I love You because You
first cast Your love on me, unworthy as I am. You chose
me and saved me. Thank You, Jesus. Amen.*

451.

Neither is there salvation in any other: for
there is none other name under heaven given
among men, whereby we must be saved.

ACTS 4:12

452.

That if thou shalt confess with thy mouth
the Lord Jesus, and shalt believe in thine
heart that God hath raised him from
the dead, thou shalt be saved.

ROMANS 10:9

453.

The LORD is good unto them that wait for him, to the soul that seeketh him. It is good that a man should both hope and quietly wait for the salvation of the LORD.

LAMENTATIONS 3:25–26

454.

For God hath not appointed us to wrath, but to obtain salvation by our Lord Jesus Christ, who died for us, that, whether we wake or sleep, we should live together with him.

1 THESSALONIANS 5:9–10

455.

For all have sinned, and come short of the glory of God; being justified freely by his grace through the redemption that is in Christ Jesus.

ROMANS 3:23–24

456.

Wherefore he is able also to save them to the
uttermost that come unto God by him, seeing
he ever liveth to make intercession for them.

HEBREWS 7:25

457.

And the Spirit and the bride say, Come. And
let him that heareth say, Come. And let him
that is athirst come. And whosoever will,
let him take the water of life freely.

REVELATION 22:17

458.

For God so loved the world, that he gave his only
begotten Son, that whosoever believeth in him
should not perish, but have everlasting life.

JOHN 3:16

459.

Not by works of righteousness which we
have done, but according to his mercy he
saved us, by the washing of regeneration,
and renewing of the Holy Ghost.

TITUS 3:5

460.

For by grace are ye saved through faith;
and that not of yourselves: it is the gift of God:
not of works, lest any man should boast.

EPHESIANS 2:8–9

STRENGTHENED

Lord, I'm exhausted by the struggle of this world. I've been trying to do it all on my own, and I've been failing miserably. I'm driven to my knees by weakness. I was about to collapse in hopeless despair—but then I looked up to heaven and I found You, the tireless Creator, the Giver of strength. Lord God, I trust You. I trust Your understanding of every impossible and strength-sapping situation that I'll ever encounter, and I'm offloading them onto the wide span of Your shoulders. Pour new strength into my weary body. I want to soar like the eagles. In Jesus' name, amen.

461.

Hast thou not known? hast thou not heard, that the everlasting God, the LORD, the Creator of the ends of the earth, fainteth not, neither is weary? there is no searching of his understanding. He giveth power to the faint; and to them that have no might he increaseth strength.

ISAIAH 40:28–29

462.

Finally, my brethren, be strong in the Lord, and in the power of his might.

EPHESIANS 6:10

463.

The Lord is my strength and song, and
he is become my salvation: he is my God,
and I will prepare him an habitation;
my father's God, and I will exalt him.

Exodus 15:2

464.

But they that wait upon the Lord shall renew
their strength; they shall mount up with
wings as eagles; they shall run, and not be
weary; and they shall walk, and not faint.

Isaiah 40:31

465.

I can do all things through
Christ which strengtheneth me.

Philippians 4:13

466.

Fear thou not; for I am with thee: be not
dismayed; for I am thy God: I will strengthen
thee; yea, I will help thee; yea, I will uphold
thee with the right hand of my righteousness.

ISAIAH 41:10

467.

And he said unto me, My grace is sufficient
for thee: for my strength is made perfect in
weakness. Most gladly therefore will I rather
glory in my infirmities, that the power
of Christ may rest upon me.

2 CORINTHIANS 12:9

468.

Seek the LORD and his strength,
seek his face continually.

1 CHRONICLES 16:11

469.

My flesh and my heart faileth: but God is the strength of my heart, and my portion for ever.

PSALM 73:26

470.

The LORD God is my strength, and he will make my feet like hinds' feet, and he will make me to walk upon mine high places.

HABAKKUK 3:19

SUSTAINED

God, I'm struggling right now. I'm feeling vulnerable and invisible. My strength is waning and I'm not sure I can go on like this. Do You see me? Where is my help? Have You forgotten me here? No. I know that You haven't. My ways are not hidden from Your sight. You shield the weak of Your flock, and You are gentle with me when I need special care. Open my eyes to the ways You are caring for me even now. You know my needs and give me just the right amount of strength. Your eye is always on me and Your hand always sustaining me. Thank You, Lord. Amen.

471.

Why sayest thou, O Jacob, and speakest,
O Israel, My way is hid from the LORD?

ISAIAH 40:27

472.

But ye are a chosen generation, a royal
priesthood, an holy nation, a peculiar people;
that ye should shew forth the praises of him
who hath called you out of darkness into his
marvellous light; which in time past were not a
people, but are now the people of God.

1 PETER 2:9–10

473.

He hath said, I will never leave
thee, nor forsake thee.

HEBREWS 13:5

474.

Give us this day our daily bread. And forgive
us our debts, as we forgive our debtors.
And lead us not into temptation, but deliver
us from evil: for thine is the kingdom,
and the power, and the glory, for ever.

MATTHEW 6:11–13

475.

Behold, the eye of the LORD is upon them that
fear him, upon them that hope in his mercy;
to deliver their soul from death, and to keep
them alive in famine. Our soul waiteth for the
LORD: he is our help and our shield.

PSALM 33:18–20

476.

But my God shall supply all your need according
to his riches in glory by Christ Jesus.

PHILIPPIANS 4:19

477.

My grace is sufficient for thee: for my
strength is made perfect in weakness.

2 CORINTHIANS 12:9

478.

And even to your old age I am he; and even to
hoar hairs will I carry you: I have made, and I
will bear; even I will carry, and will deliver you.
To whom will ye liken me, and make me equal,
and compare me, that we may be like?

ISAIAH 46:4–5

479.

I laid me down and slept; I awaked;
for the Lord sustained me.

Psalm 3:5

480.

Let all the earth fear the Lord: let all the
inhabitants of the world stand in awe of
him. For he spake, and it was done;
he commanded, and it stood fast.

Psalm 33:8–9

TAUGHT

*God, You never stop teaching me more about Yourself.
Just when I think that I have a good grasp on who You
are, You blow my mind with Your absolute limitlessness.
And You are a patient instructor, slowly building on the
foundation of my knowledge. You desire to be known
by me, and You sent Your Holy Spirit to be my teacher.
Continue to reveal Yourself to me in new ways. I'm
fascinated and amazed by Your complexity and depth
and precision. I want to know more! In the name of
Jesus I pray, amen.*

481.

But the Comforter, which is the Holy Ghost,
whom the Father will send in my name, he shall
teach you all things, and bring all things to your
remembrance, whatsoever I have said unto you.

John 14:26

482.

All scripture is given by inspiration of God,
and is profitable for doctrine, for reproof,
for correction, for instruction in righteousness:
that the man of God may be perfect,
thoroughly furnished unto all good works.

2 Timothy 3:16–17

483.

The law of the LORD is perfect,
converting the soul: the testimony of the
LORD is sure, making wise the simple.

PSALM 19:7

484.

But continue thou in the things which thou
hast learned and hast been assured of,
knowing of whom thou hast learned them.

2 TIMOTHY 3:14

485.

The heavens declare the glory of God;
and the firmament sheweth his handywork.
Day unto day uttereth speech, and night
unto night sheweth knowledge.

PSALM 19:1–2

486.

It is written in the prophets,
And they shall be all taught of God.

<small>John 6:45</small>

487.

For the invisible things of him from the creation
of the world are clearly seen, being understood by
the things that are made, even his eternal power
and Godhead; so that they are without excuse.

<small>Romans 1:20</small>

488.

But ask now the beasts, and they shall teach thee;
and the fowls of the air, and they shall tell thee:
or speak to the earth, and it shall teach thee: and
the fishes of the sea shall declare unto thee. Who
knoweth not in all these that the hand of the Lord
hath wrought this?

<small>Job 12:7–9</small>

489.
He loveth righteousness and judgment:
the earth is full of the goodness of the LORD.
PSALM 33:5

490.
For whom the LORD loveth he correcteth;
even as a father the son in whom he delighteth.
Happy is the man that findeth wisdom,
and the man that getteth understanding.
PROVERBS 3:12–13

TRANSFORMED

Father, knowing You has changed me. You have taken this useless lump of unformed, dried-up clay and transformed me into a thing of beauty. You've stripped away all the excess, giving my life purpose and making me a magnificent vessel for You. I'm no longer dead, but alive in Your love and grace. I'm not the same person who existed in a state of hopeless despair. You've changed the way I think and renewed my mind. I have a fresh perspective and my thoughts are consumed with You. Now I live a new life for You. Thank You, Lord. In Jesus' name, amen.

491.

And be not conformed to this world: but be ye transformed by the renewing of your mind, that ye may prove what is that good, and acceptable, and perfect, will of God.

ROMANS 12:2

492.

Therefore if any man be in Christ, he is a new creature: old things are passed away; behold, all things are become new.

2 CORINTHIANS 5:17

493.

Put on the new man, which after God is
created in righteousness and true holiness.

<small>EPHESIANS 4:24</small>

494.

Beloved, now are we the sons of God, and it
doth not yet appear what we shall be: but we
know that, when he shall appear, we shall be
like him; for we shall see him as he is.

<small>1 JOHN 3:2</small>

495.

And you, that were sometime alienated and
enemies in your mind by wicked works, yet
now hath he reconciled in the body of his flesh
through death, to present you holy and
unblameable and unreproveable in his sight.

<small>COLOSSIANS 1:21–22</small>

496.

That being justified by his grace, we should be
made heirs according to the hope of eternal life.

TITUS 3:7

497.

A new heart also will I give you, and a new
spirit will I put within you: and I will take
away the stony heart out of your flesh,
and I will give you an heart of flesh.

EZEKIEL 36:26

498.

Create in me a clean heart, O God;
and renew a right spirit within me.

PSALM 51:10

499.

But we all, with open face beholding as in a glass the glory of the Lord, are changed into the same image from glory to glory, even as by the Spirit of the Lord.

2 Corinthians 3:18

500.

Being confident of this very thing, that he which hath begun a good work in you will perform it until the day of Jesus Christ.

Philippians 1:6

MORE BIBLE PROMISE
BOOK® EDITIONS

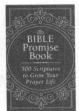

The Bible Promise Book®:
500 Scriptures to Grow Your Prayer Life

Barbour's Bible Promise Books® are perennial bestsellers, with millions of copies in print. Now, *The Bible Promise Book®* is available in an inspiring edition featuring 500 scripture selections plus encouraging prayer starters to help you grow in your prayer life. With 50 topics related to the theme of prayer—including Confidence, Thankfulness, Faith, Trust, Praise, Courage, Joy, and more—you can quickly and easily locate a topic that will speak to your needs.
Paperback / 978-1-68322-863-9 / $5.99

The Bible Promise Book®:
500 Scriptures to Bless a Woman's Heart

The Bible Promise Book® is also available in a lovely paperback edition featuring 500 scripture selections plus encouraging prayer starters to bless women's hearts. With 50 topics that matter most—including Comfort, Love, Faith, Worry, Worship, Courage, Joy, and Contentment—readers can quickly and easily locate a topic of importance for their situation.
Paperback / 978-1-68322-729-8 / $5.99